Grammar +Plus Writing

START

1

DARAKWON

저자 약력

전지원

미국 오리건 주립대 Linguistics 석사
(현) 한국 외국어대학교 외국어연수 평가원 영어 전임강사
〈내공 중학 영작문〉(다락원), 〈Grammar Mate〉(다락원),
〈Grammar's Cool〉(YBM), 〈빠르게 잡는 영문법〉(천재교육) 등 다수의 교재 공저

박혜영

미국 하와이 주립대 Second Language Studies 석사
(현) 한국 외국어대학교 외국어연수 평가원 영어 전임강사
〈내공 중학 영작문〉(다락원), 〈Grammar Mate〉(다락원),
〈Grammar's Cool〉(YBM), 〈빠르게 잡는 영문법〉(천재교육) 등 다수의 교재 공저

Grammar Plus Writing START 1

지은이 전지원, 박혜영
펴낸이 정규도
펴낸곳 (주)다락원

개정판 1쇄 발행 2023년 12월 11일

편집 서정아, 홍인표, 안혜원
디자인 김민지, 포레스트
영문 감수 Michael A. Putlack

다락원 경기도 파주시 문발로 211
내용문의 (02) 736-2031 내선 503
구입문의 (02) 736-2031 내선 250~252
Fax (02) 732-2037
출판등록 1977년 9월 16일 제406-2008-000007호

ISBN 978-89-277-8068-7 64740
     978-89-277-8067-0 64740(set)

http://www.darakwon.co.kr

다락원 홈페이지를 방문하시면 상세한 출판 정보와 함께 동영상 강좌,
MP3 자료 등의 다양한 어학 정보를 얻으실 수 있습니다.

Grammar +Plus Writing

START

1

STRUCTURES 구성과 특징

Grammar +lus Writing START 시리즈는

- 각 문법 사항을 이해하기 쉽게 구성하여 기초 영문법을 쉽고 재미있게 학습할 수 있습니다.
- 학습한 문법 요소를 영작과 연계하여 문법 지식과 영작 능력을 동시에 향상시킬 수 있습니다.
- 학교 내신 및 서술형 문제에 효과적으로 대비할 수 있습니다.

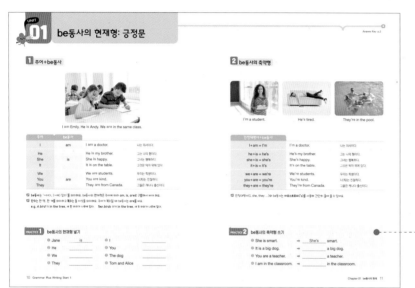

문법 설명

사진과 함께 대표 예문을 확인하고, 표를 통해 핵심 문법 사항을 간략히 정리할 수 있어요.

PRACTICE

문제를 통해 학습한 내용을 이해했는지 바로 체크해볼 수 있어요.

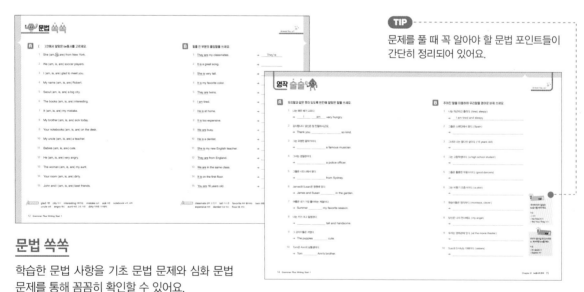

TIP

문제를 풀 때 꼭 알아야 할 문법 포인트들이 간단히 정리되어 있어요.

문법 쏙쏙

학습한 문법 사항을 기초 문법 문제와 심화 문법 문제를 통해 꼼꼼히 확인할 수 있어요.

영작 술술

학습한 문법 사항을 영작과 연계하여 연습할 수 있어요. 영작 술술 A는 본격적인 영작에 들어가기 전 준비 과정으로 활용할 수 있으며, B에서는 완전한 영어 문장을 써 볼 수 있어요.

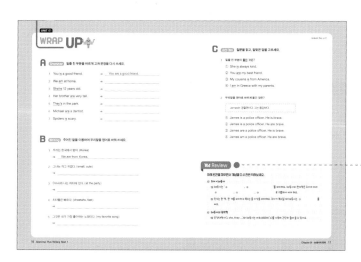

WRAP UP

각 Unit에서 배운 내용을 문법·영작·내신 문제를 통해 다시 한번 정리할 수 있어요.

개념 REVIEW

꼭 기억해야 할 중요 문법 개념들을 빈칸 채우기를 통해 복습할 수 있어요.

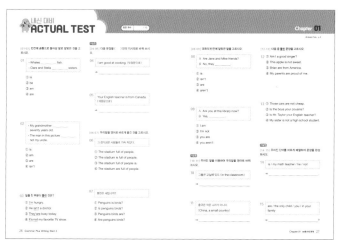

내신 대비 ACTUAL TEST

챕터가 끝날 때마다 배운 내용을 종합적으로 확인해 볼 수 있어요. 다양한 내신 유형과 서술형 문제에 대비할 수 있으며, 자신의 실력을 평가할 수 있어요.

WORKBOOK

1 Grammar & Writing Practice

본책에서 학습한 내용을 A에서는 문법 문제, B에서는 영작 문제를 통해 복습할 수 있어요.

2 Word Practice

본문에서 쓰인 필수 어휘를 듣고 따라 쓰며, 영작에 유용한 단어들을 복습하고 정리할 수 있어요.

온라인 부가자료 | www.darakwon.co.kr

다락원 홈페이지에서 무료로 부가자료를 다운로드하거나 웹에서 이용할 수 있습니다.

CONTENTS 목차

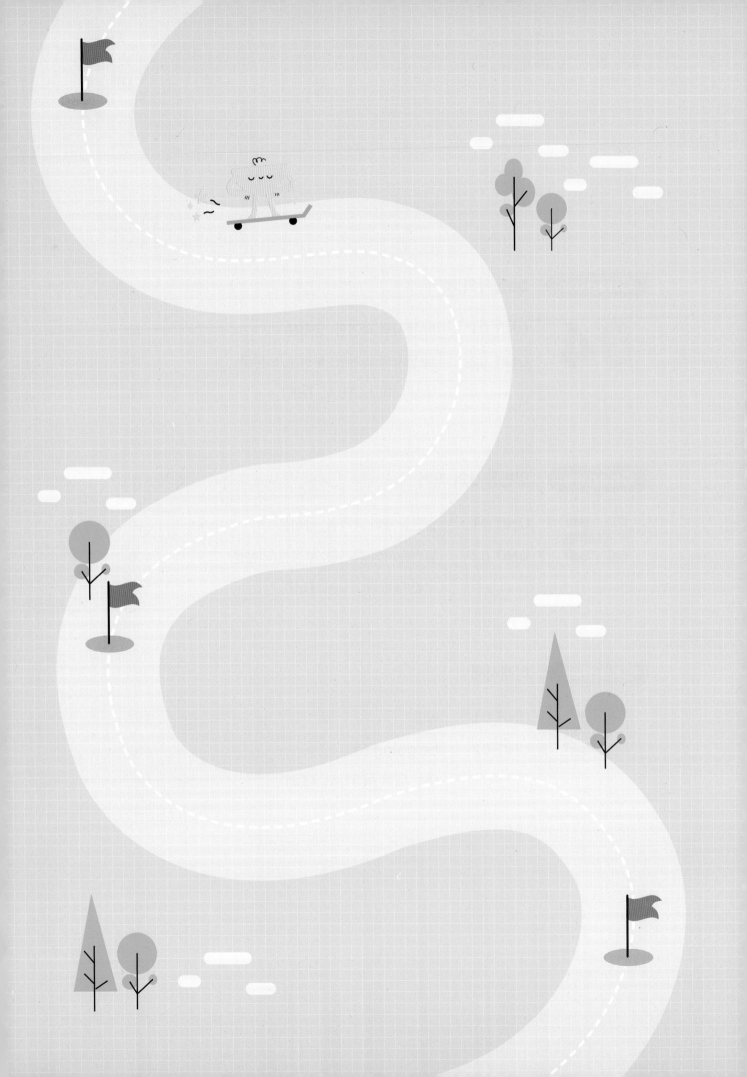

01

be동사의 현재

학습목표

1 be동사의 의미와 주어에 따른 be동사의 형태를 알아봐요.

2 be동사 현재형 문장의 부정문과 의문문 만드는 법을 알아봐요.

UNIT 01 be동사의 현재형: 긍정문

1 주어+be동사

I **am** Emily. He **is** Andy. We **are** in the same class.

주어	be동사		
I	am	I **am** a doctor.	나는 의사이다.
He She It	is	He **is** my brother. She **is** happy. It **is** on the table.	그는 나의 형이다. 그녀는 행복하다. 그것은 탁자 위에 있다.
We You They	are	We **are** students. You **are** kind. They **are** from Canada.	우리는 학생이다. 너(희)는 친절하다. 그들은 캐나다 출신이다.

☑ **be동사**는 '~이다, (~에) 있다'를 의미해요. be동사의 현재형은 주어에 따라 **am, is, are**로 구별해서 써야 해요.

☑ **단수**는 한 명, 한 개를 의미하고 **복수**는 둘 이상을 의미해요. 주어가 복수일 때 be동사는 **are**를 써요.
  e.g. *A bird* is in the tree. 새 한 마리가 나무에 있다. *Two birds* are in the tree. 새 두 마리가 나무에 있다.

PRACTICE 1 be동사의 현재형 넣기

❶ Jane _____is_____   ❺ I _____

❷ He _____   ❻ You _____

❸ We _____   ❼ The dog _____

❹ They _____   ❽ Tom and Alice _____

2 be동사의 축약형

I'm a student.

He's tired.

They're in the pool.

인칭대명사+be동사

I+am = I'm	I'm a doctor.	나는 의사이다.
he+is = he's	He's my brother.	그는 나의 형이다.
she+is = she's	She's happy.	그녀는 행복하다.
it+is = it's	It's on the table.	그것은 탁자 위에 있다.
we+are = we're	We're students.	우리는 학생이다.
you+are = you're	You're kind.	너(희)는 친절하다.
they+are = they're	They're from Canada.	그들은 캐나다 출신이다.

☑ 인칭대명사(I, she, they ...)와 be동사는 **아포스트로피('s)**를 사용해 간단히 줄여 쓸 수 있어요.

PRACTICE 2 be동사의 축약형 쓰기

① She is smart. ➡ __She's__ smart.

② It is a big dog. ➡ _____ a big dog.

③ You are a teacher. ➡ _____ a teacher.

④ I am in the classroom. ➡ _____ in the classroom.

문법 쏙쏙

A ( ) 안에서 알맞은 be동사를 고르세요.

1 She (am, is, are) from New York.

2 We (am, is, are) soccer players.

3 I (am, is, are) glad to meet you.

4 My name (am, is, are) Robert.

5 Seoul (am, is, are) a big city.

6 The books (am, is, are) interesting.

7 It (am, is, are) my mistake.

8 My brother (am, is, are) sick today.

9 Your notebooks (am, is, are) on the desk.

10 My uncle (am, is, are) a teacher.

11 Babies (am, is, are) cute.

12 He (am, is, are) very angry.

13 The woman (am, is, are) my aunt.

14 Your room (am, is, are) dirty.

15 John and I (am, is, are) best friends.

WORDS glad 기쁜 city 도시 interesting 재미있는 mistake 실수 sick 아픈 notebook 노트, 공책
uncle 삼촌 angry 화난 aunt 숙모, 고모, 이모 dirty 더러운, 지저분한

B 밑줄 친 부분의 줄임말을 쓰세요.

1 <u>They are</u> my classmates. → They're

2 <u>It is</u> a great song. →

3 <u>She is</u> very tall. →

4 <u>It is</u> my favorite color. →

5 <u>They are</u> twins. →

6 <u>I am</u> tired. →

7 <u>He is</u> at home. →

8 <u>It is</u> too expensive. →

9 <u>We are</u> busy. →

10 <u>He is</u> a dentist. →

11 <u>She is</u> my new English teacher. →

12 <u>They are</u> from England. →

13 <u>We are</u> in the same class. →

14 <u>It is</u> on the first floor. →

15 <u>You are</u> 16 years old. →

WORDS classmate 급우, 반 친구　tall 키가 큰　favorite 매우 좋아하는　twin 쌍둥이　tired 피곤한
expensive 비싼　dentist 치과 의사　floor 층, 바닥

영작 술술

A 우리말과 같은 뜻이 되도록 빈칸에 알맞은 말을 쓰세요.

1 나는 매우 배가 고프다.

→ ____I____ ____am____ very hungry.

2 감사합니다. 당신은 참 친절하시군요.

→ Thank you. _____ _____ so kind.

3 그는 유명한 음악가이다.

→ _____ _____ a famous musician.

4 그녀는 경찰관이다.

→ _____ _____ a police officer.

5 그들은 시드니에서 왔다.

→ _____ _____ from Sydney.

6 James와 Susan은 정원에 있다.

→ James and Susan _____ in the garden.

7 여름은 내가 가장 좋아하는 계절이다.

→ Summer _____ my favorite season.

8 너는 키가 크고 잘생겼다.

→ _____ _____ tall and handsome.

9 그 강아지들은 귀엽다.

→ The puppies _____ cute.

10 Tom은 Ann의 남동생이다.

→ Tom _____ Ann's brother.

B 주어진 말을 이용하여 우리말을 영어로 바꿔 쓰세요.

1   나는 피곤하고 졸리다. (tired, sleepy)

   ➡   I am tired and sleepy.

2   그들은 스페인에서 왔다. (Spain)

   ➡   _____

3   그녀와 나는 열다섯 살이다. (15 years old)

   ➡   _____

4   그는 고등학생이다. (a high school student)

   ➡   _____

5   그들은 훌륭한 무용수이다. (good dancers)

   ➡   _____

6   그는 비행기 조종사이다. (a pilot)

   ➡   _____

TIP 1

주어에 따라 알맞은 be동사를 써야 해요.

e.g.
- I am
- He/She/It is
- We/You/They are

7   원숭이들은 영리하다. (monkeys, clever)

   ➡   _____

8   당신은 나의 천사예요. (my angel)

   ➡   _____

TIP 2

주어가 명사일 때 단수이면 is, 복수이면 are를 써요.

e.g.
- An apple is
- Apples are

9   우리는 영화관에 있다. (at the movie theater)

   ➡   _____

10   Sue과 Emily는 자매이다. (sisters)

   ➡   _____

WRAP UP

A Grammar 밑줄 친 부분을 바르게 고쳐 문장을 다시 쓰세요.

1 You <u>is</u> a good friend. ➡ You are a good friend.

2 We <u>am</u> at home. ➡ _____

3 <u>She're</u> 12 years old. ➡ _____

4 Her brother <u>are</u> very tall. ➡ _____

5 <u>They's</u> in the park. ➡ _____

6 Michael <u>are</u> a dentist. ➡ _____

7 Spiders <u>is</u> scary. ➡ _____

B Writing 주어진 말을 이용하여 우리말을 영어로 바꿔 쓰세요.

1 우리는 한국에서 왔어. (Korea)

➡ We are from Korea. _____

2 그녀는 작고 귀엽다. (small, cute)

➡ _____

3 Steve와 나는 파티에 있다. (at the party)

➡ _____

4 치타들은 빠르다. (cheetahs, fast)

➡ _____

5 그것은 내가 가장 좋아하는 노래이다. (my favorite song)

➡ _____

C 내신 대비 질문을 읽고, 알맞은 답을 고르세요.

1 밑줄 친 부분이 틀린 것은?

① She <u>is</u> always kind.

② You <u>are</u> my best friend.

③ My cousins <u>is</u> from America.

④ I <u>am</u> in Greece with my parents.

2 우리말을 영어로 바르게 옮긴 것은?

> James는 경찰관이다. 그는 용감하다.

① James is a police officer. He is brave.

② James is a police officer. He are brave.

③ James are a police officer. He is brave.

④ James am a police officer. He are brave.

개념 Review

아래 빈칸을 채우면서 개념을 다시 한번 익혀보세요.

❶ **주어 + be동사**

☑ be동사는 ' ❶   , ❷   '를 의미해요. be동사의 현재형은 주어에 따라

     ❸   , ❹   , ❺   로 구별해서 써야 해요.

☑ 단수는 한 명, 한 개를 의미하고 복수는 둘 이상을 의미해요. 주어가 복수일 때 be동사는 ❻   를

     써요.

❷ **be동사의 축약형**

☑ 인칭대명사(I, she, they ...)와 be동사는 아포스트로피(’s)를 사용해 간단히 줄여 쓸 수 있어요.

UNIT 02 be동사의 현재형: 부정문 / 의문문

1 부정문

I **am not** sad.

The box **is not** small.

주어	be동사+not		
I	am not	I **am not** a good singer.	나는 노래를 잘 못한다.
He She It	is not (= isn't)	He **is not** Mr. Green. She **is not** hungry. It **is not** in the box.	그는 Green 선생님이 아니다. 그녀는 배가 고프지 않다. 그것은 상자 안에 없다.
We You They	are not (= aren't)	We **are not** late. You **are not** at home. They **are not** actors.	우리는 늦지 않았다. 너(희)는 집에 없다. 그들은 배우가 아니다.

☑ be동사의 부정문은 be동사 뒤에 **not**을 붙이면 돼요.

☑ is not은 **isn't**로, are not은 **aren't**로 줄여 쓸 수 있어요. 단, am not은 amn't로 줄여 쓸 수 없어요.

☑ be동사의 부정문은 「인칭대명사+be동사」의 축약형 뒤에 **not**을 붙여 쓰기도 해요.
   e.g. I**'m not** a good singer. / He**'s not** Mr. Green. / We**'re not** late.

PRACTICE 1 be동사의 부정문 만들기

❶ He is lazy. → <u>He is not lazy.</u>

❷ It is my cellphone. → <u> </u>

❸ We are in the kitchen. → <u> </u>

❹ They are friends. → <u> </u>

2 의문문

be동사+주어 ~?		긍정의 대답	부정의 대답
Am I a good singer?	내가 노래를 잘 하니?	Yes, you **are**.	No, you **aren't**.
Are you at home?	너는 집에 있니?	Yes, I **am**.	No, I'm **not**.
Is he Mr. Green?	그는 Green 선생님이니?	Yes, he **is**.	No, he **isn't**.
Is she hungry?	그녀는 배가 고프니?	Yes, she **is**.	No, she **isn't**.
Is it in the box?	그것은 상자 안에 있니?	Yes, it **is**.	No, it **isn't**.
Are we late?	우리는 늦었니?	Yes, you **are**.	No, you **aren't**.
Are you at home?	너희는 집에 있니?	Yes, we **are**.	No, we **aren't**.
Are they actors?	그들은 배우니?	Yes, they **are**.	No, they **aren't**.

☑ be동사의 의문문은 주어와 be동사의 순서를 바꾸고, 문장 끝에 물음표(?)를 붙여요.

PRACTICE 2 be 동사의 의문문 만들기

❶ She is a nurse. ➡ _Is she a nurse?_

❷ You are thirsty. ➡ _____

❸ The house is big. ➡ _____

❹ They are at the library. ➡ _____

문법 쏙쏙

A 다음 문장을 부정문으로 바꿔 쓰세요.

1 It is an easy question.

➡   It is not an easy question.

2 He is kind to people.

➡

3 I am afraid of snakes.

➡

4 She is at school now.

➡

5 They are interested in movies.

➡

6 The window is open.

➡

7 The books are on the table.

➡

8 The sun is bright today.

➡

9 Your birthday is in April.

➡

10 Ann is good at singing.

➡

WORDS   question 질문, 문제   people 사람들   be afraid of ~을 두려워[무서워]하다   snake 뱀   be interested in
~에 관심[흥미]이 있다   bright 밝은   birthday 생일   April 4월   be good at ~을 잘하다

B 다음 문장을 의문문으로 바꿔 쓰세요.

1 The shoes are too big.

→ _Are the shoes too big?_

2 The diamond ring is expensive.

→ _____

3 Tomatoes are vegetables.

→ _____

4 The milk is in the refrigerator.

→ _____

5 You are a soccer fan.

→ _____

6 She is still in bed.

→ _____

7 We are late for the movie.

→ _____

8 The post office is open on Saturdays.

→ _____

9 Italy is famous for operas.

→ _____

10 Your brother's name is Chris.

→ _____

 WORDS   shoes 신발   diamond ring 다이아몬드 반지   tomato 토마토   vegetable 야채, 채소
refrigerator 냉장고   still 여전히, 아직도   post office 우체국   Saturday 토요일
be famous for ~로 유명하다   opera 오페라

A 우리말과 같은 뜻이 되도록 빈칸에 알맞은 말을 쓰세요.

1 그녀는 너의 친구니?

→ _____Is_____ _____she_____ your friend?

2 나는 스포츠에 관심이 없다.

→ I _____ _____ interested in sports.

3 그것은 너의 잘못이 아니다.

→ It _____ _____ your fault.

4 내가 맞아 아니면 틀려?

→ _____ _____ right or wrong?

5 그 영화는 재미가 없다.

→ The movie _____ _____ interesting.

6 그들은 호주에서 왔니?

→ _____ _____ from Australia?

7 그는 거실에 없다.

→ He _____ _____ in the living room.

8 너는 지금 한가하니?

→ _____ _____ free now?

9 너의 부모님은 엄격하시니?

→ _____ your parents strict?

10 Paul과 나는 같은 반이 아니다.

→ Paul and I _____ _____ in the same class.

B 주어진 말을 이용하여 우리말을 영어로 바꿔 쓰세요.

1 그 열쇠들은 탁자 위에 없다. (the keys, on the table)

➡ The keys are not on the table.

2 너의 가방은 파란색이니? (your bag, blue)

➡

3 나는 거짓말쟁이가 아니다. (a liar)

➡

4 그들은 결혼하지 않았다. (married)

➡

5 너는 개를 무서워하니? (be afraid of, dogs)

➡

6 그녀는 빨리 달리지 못한다. (a fast runner)

➡

TIP 1

be동사의 부정문은 be동사 뒤에 not을 붙이면 돼요.

e.g.
- I am not
- He is not
- They are not

7 이 상자는 무겁지 않다. (this box, heavy)

➡

8 우리는 목이 마르지 않다. (thirsty)

➡

TIP 2

be동사의 의문문은 be동사가 주어 앞에 와요.

e.g.
- Am I ~?
- Is he ~?
- Are they ~?

9 Mina와 Susie는 자매입니까? (sisters)

➡

10 그녀의 이름은 Kate니? (her name)

➡

WRAP UP

A Grammar 밑줄 친 부분을 바르게 고쳐 문장을 다시 쓰세요.

1 He is kind to children? ➡ Is he kind to children?

2 Joe not is fat. ➡ _____

3 Are Susan angry with me? ➡ _____

4 Elephants is not light. ➡ _____

5 Is they twins? ➡ _____

6 I not a good dancer. ➡ _____

7 Don't worry. You is not alone. ➡ _____

B Writing 주어진 말을 이용하여 우리말을 영어로 바꿔 쓰세요.

1 Amy는 오늘 아픈가요? (sick)

➡ Is Amy sick today?

2 그들은 열다섯 살이 아니다. (15 years old)

➡ _____

3 John과 Amy는 도서관에 없다. (at the library)

➡ _____

4 그 박물관은 일요일에 문을 엽니까? (the museum, open, on Sundays)

➡ _____

5 너의 아버지는 선생님이시니? (your father, a teacher)

➡ _____

C 내신 대비 질문을 읽고, 알맞은 답을 고르세요.

1 밑줄 친 부분이 틀린 것은?

① She <u>isn't</u> at home.

② I <u>amn't</u> a good singer.

③ The trees <u>aren't</u> tall.

④ <u>They're not</u> interested in sports.

2 우리말을 영어로 바르게 옮긴 것은?

> Carl와 Lily는 학교에 있니?

① Carl and Lily is at school?

② Is Carl and Lily at school?

③ Carl and Lily are at school?

④ Are Carl and Lily at school?

개념 Review

아래 빈칸을 채우면서 개념을 다시 한번 익혀보세요.

❶ **be동사의 현재형: 부정문**

☑ be동사의 부정문은 be동사 뒤에 ❶   을 붙이면 돼요.

☑ is not은 ❷   로, are not은 ❸   로 줄여 쓸 수 있어요. 단, am not은 amn't로 줄여 쓸 수 없어요.

☑ be동사의 부정문은 「인칭대명사＋be동사」의 축약형 뒤에 not을 붙여 쓰기도 해요.

    e.g. I**'m not** a good singer. / He**'s not** Mr. Green. / We**'re not** late.

❷ **be동사의 현재형: 의문문**

☑ be동사의 의문문은 ❹   와 be동사의 순서를 바꾸고, 문장 끝에 ❺   를 붙여요.

[01-02] 빈칸에 공통으로 들어갈 말로 알맞은 것을 고르시오.

01

- Whales _____ fish.
- Clara and Stella _____ sisters.

① is
② be
③ am
④ are

02

- My grandmother _____ seventy years old.
- The man in this picture _____ not my uncle.

① is
② am
③ are
④ isn't

03 밑줄 친 부분이 틀린 것은?

① I'm hungry.
② He isn't a doctor.
③ They'are busy today.
④ It's not my favorite TV show.

[04-05] 다음 문장을 ( ) 안의 지시대로 바꿔 쓰시오.

04

I am good at cooking. (부정문으로)

➡ _____

05

Your English teacher is from Canada. (의문문으로)

➡ _____

[06-07] 우리말을 영어로 바르게 옮긴 것을 고르시오.

06

그 경기장은 사람들로 가득 차있다.

① The stadium full of people.
② The stadium is full of people.
③ The stadium full of people is.
④ The stadium are full of people.

07

펭귄은 새입니까?

① Penguins is birds?
② Is penguins birds?
③ Penguins birds are?
④ Are penguins birds?

Chapter 01

Answer Key p.4

[08-09] 대화의 빈칸에 알맞은 말을 고르시오.

08

> A Are Jane and Mike friends?
> B No, they _____.

① is

② isn't

③ are

④ aren't

09

> A Are you at the library now?
> B Yes, _____.

① I am

② I'm not

③ you are

④ you aren't

서술형

[10-11] 주어진 말을 이용하여 우리말을 영어로 바꿔 쓰시오.

10

> 그들은 교실에 있다. (in the classroom)

➡ _____

11

> 중국은 작은 나라가 아니다.
> (China, a small country)

➡ _____

[12-13] 다음 중 **틀린** 문장을 고르시오.

12 ① Am I a good singer?

② This apple is not sweet.

③ Brian are from America.

④ My parents are proud of me.

13 ① Those cars are not cheap.

② Is the boys your cousins?

③ Is Mr. Taylor your English teacher?

④ My sister is not a high school student.

서술형

[14-15] 주어진 단어를 바르게 배열하여 문장을 완성 하시오.

14

> is / my math teacher / he / not

➡ _____.

15

> are / the only child / you / in your family

➡ _____?

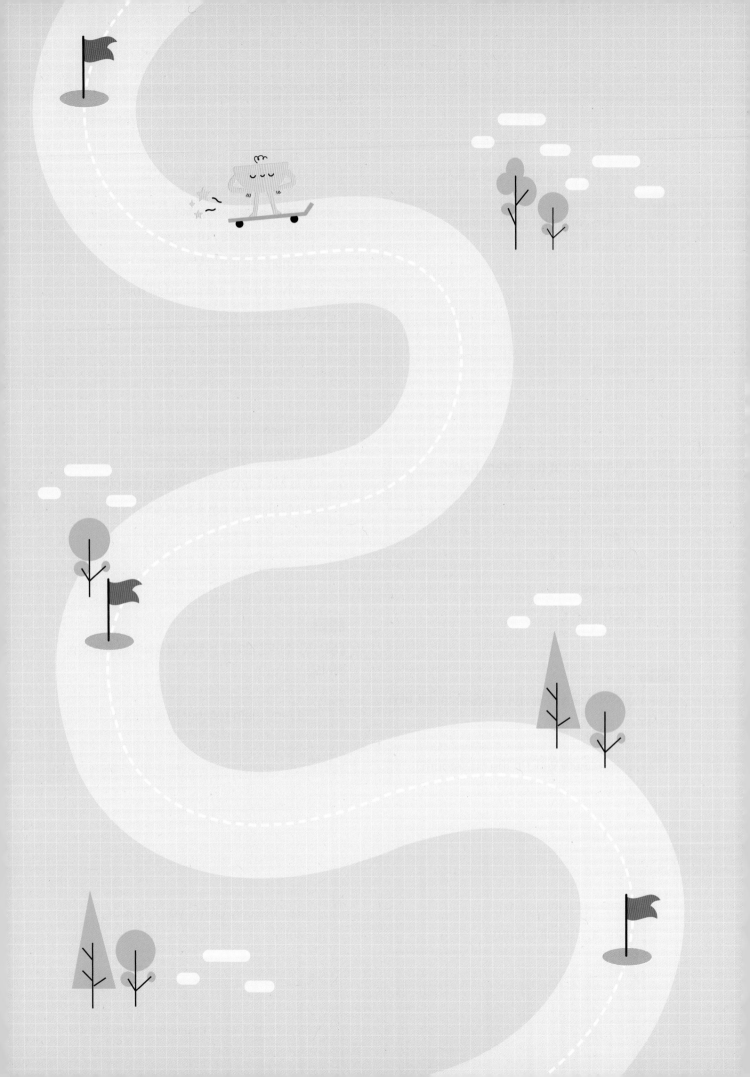

02

일반동사의 현재

학습목표

1   일반동사의 의미와 주어에 따른 일반동사의 형태를 알아봐요.

2   일반동사 현재형 문장의 부정문과 의문문 만드는 법을 알아봐요.

일반동사의 현재형: 긍정문

1 주어 + 일반동사

I **like** ice cream.

They **walk** to school every day.

주어	일반동사		
I You We They	동사원형	I **live** in a city. You **speak** English. We **go** to school. They **play** soccer.	나는 도시에 산다. 너(희)는 영어를 말한다. 우리는 학교에 다닌다. 그들은 축구를 한다.
He She It	동사원형+-s/es	He **works** at a bank. She **likes** music. It **runs** very fast.	그는 은행에서 일한다. 그녀는 음악을 좋아한다. 그것은 매우 빨리 달린다.

☑ **일반동사**란 go, eat, have 등과 같이 주어의 동작이나 상태를 나타내는 동사예요.

☑ 일반동사 현재형의 긍정문은 주어가 **3인칭 단수**(he, she, it, 단수 명사)일 때 동사원형 뒤에 **-s/es**를 붙여요.

PRACTICE 1 일반동사 현재형의 긍정문 만들기

❶ I ____watch____ TV in the evening. (watch)

❷ You _____ glasses. (wear)

❸ He _____ breakfast at 8 o'clock. (eat)

❹ My cat _____ in my bedroom. (sleep)

2 일반동사의 3인칭 단수형

He **studies** at the library.

Emma **has** a twin sister.

동사의 종류	규칙		
대부분의 동사	+-s	run → run**s**	like → like**s**
-o, -ch, -sh, -ss, -x로 끝나는 동사	+-es	do → do**es** teach → teach**es** pass → pass**es**	go → go**es** wash → wash**es** fix → fix**es**
「자음+y」로 끝나는 동사	y를 i로 고치고 +-es	cry → cri**es**	study → studi**es**
「모음+y」로 끝나는 동사	+-s	enjoy → enjoy**s**	play → play**s**
have	불규칙 변화	have → **has**	

☑ 대부분의 동사 뒤에는 **-s**를 붙이고, -o, -ch, -sh, -ss, -x로 끝나는 동사 뒤에는 **-es**를 붙여요.

☑ 「자음+y」로 끝나는 동사는 **y를 i로 고치고 -es**를 붙여요. 「모음+y」로 끝나면 **-s**만 붙여요.

☑ have는 불규칙 동사로 **has**로 바꿔요.

PRACTICE 2 일반동사의 3인칭 단수형 만들기

❶ sleep   ➡   ___sleeps___   ❺ make   ➡   _____

❷ talk   ➡   _____   ❻ fly   ➡   _____

❸ watch   ➡   _____   ❼ buy   ➡   _____

❹ brush   ➡   _____   ❽ have   ➡   _____

문법 쏙쏙

A ( ) 안에서 알맞은 것을 고르세요.

1 Frank (drive, drives) a taxi.

2 Dogs (love, loves) bones.

3 The museum (open, opens) at 10:00 a.m.

4 We (go, goes) for a walk after lunch.

5 Mary (have, has) a sister and two brothers.

6 You (have, has) a beautiful garden.

7 The boys (play, plays) soccer every day.

8 Jack and Cindy (walk, walks) to school.

9 My best friend (live, lives) in my town.

10 The train (leave, leaves) every hour.

11 I (like, likes) chocolate milk.

12 The desk (cost, costs) 100 dollars.

13 Janet always (forget, forgets) her keys.

14 Andy (exercise, exercises) every day.

15 My parents (go, goes) to church on Sundays.

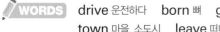 **WORDS**   drive 운전하다   born 뼈   go for a walk 산책하러 가다   lunch 점심 식사   beautiful 아름다운
town 마을, 소도시   leave 떠나다   cost (비용이) ~이다   forget 잊다, 잊어버리다   exercise 운동하다
go to church 교회에 가다

B 주어진 동사를 현재형으로 바꿔 쓰세요.

1 The shop ___closes___ at 8:00 p.m. (close)

2 Mr. Miller _____ in New York. (work)

3 We _____ swimming in summer. (enjoy)

4 I _____ my homework every day. (do)

5 Some babies _____ all the time. (cry)

6 Teachers _____ students in class. (help)

7 He _____ English every day. (study)

8 Emily _____ her hair every morning. (wash)

9 Tom and I _____ to school by bus. (go)

10 The singer _____ a beautiful voice. (have)

11 Children _____ toys. (like)

12 My grandfather _____ books every day. (read)

13 Mr. Johnson _____ art. (teach)

14 Ethan _____ his teeth twice a day. (brush)

15 I _____ up at 7 o'clock in the morning. (get)

 WORDS   enjoy 즐기다   do one's homework 숙제를 하다   cry 울다   help 돕다   all the time 항상
wash one's hair 머리를 감다   by bus 버스로   voice 목소리   brush one's teeth 이를 닦다
twice a day 하루에 두 번   get up 일어나다

A 우리말과 같은 뜻이 되도록 빈칸에 알맞은 말을 쓰세요.

1   그들은 부산에 산다.

→ They _____live_____ in Busan.

2   나는 일요일 아침에는 늦게 일어난다.

→ I _____ up late on Sunday morning.

3   Mike는 밤 11시에 자러 간다.

→ Mike _____ to bed at 11:00 p.m.

4   Grace는 아침에 커피를 마신다.

→ Grace _____ coffee in the morning.

5   Bob은 매일 신문을 읽는다.

→ Bob _____ the newspaper every day.

6   그는 보통 주말에는 집에 머문다.

→ He usually _____ at home on weekends.

7   나의 가족과 나는 저녁에 TV를 본다.

→ My family and I _____ TV in the evening.

8   그녀는 매주 금요일 자신의 친구들을 만난다.

→ She _____ her friends every Friday.

9   나에게는 개 한 마리가 있는데, 그것은 많이 먹는다.

→ I _____ a dog, and it _____ a lot.

10 그는 차 안에서 라디오를 듣는다.

→ He _____ to the radio in the car.

Hint

drink	eat
get	go
have	listen
meet	read
stay	watch

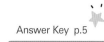

B 주어진 말을 이용하여 우리말을 영어로 바꿔 쓰세요.

1 Kate는 스페인어를 매우 잘 한다. (speak Spanish, very well)

→   Kate speaks Spanish very well.

2 John은 학교에서 수학을 가르친다. (teach math, at school)

→

3 고양이들은 생선을 좋아한다. (cats, fish)

→

4 그녀는 아침 일찍 일어난다. (get up, early in the morning)

→

5 그는 보통 아침 식사를 거른다. (usually, skip breakfast)

→

6 Betty는 10시에 자러 간다. (go to bed, at 10 o'clock)

→

7 우리는 공원에서 축구를 한다. (play soccer, in the park)

→

8 나는 방과 후에 숙제를 한다. (do my homework, after school)

→

9 Sam은 멋진 컴퓨터를 가지고 있다. (a nice computer)

→

10 그들은 저녁에 TV를 본다 (watch TV, in the evening)

→

TIP 1

주어가 3인칭 단수(he, she, it, 단수 명사)이면 일반동사에 -s/es를 붙여 현재형을 만들어요.

e.g.
- He works.
- It runs.
- The baby cries.

TIP 2

'보통, 평소에'라는 의미의 usually는 주로 일반동사 앞에 위치해요.

e.g.
- Jane usually has breakfast.

WRAP UP

A Grammar 밑줄 친 부분을 바르게 고쳐 문장을 다시 쓰세요. (단, 현재형으로 쓸 것)

1 Sally <u>do</u> her homework. ➡ Sally does her homework.

2 I <u>goes</u> to school every day. ➡ _____

3 My dad <u>cook</u> very well. ➡ _____

4 You <u>reads</u> a lot of books. ➡ _____

5 Students <u>likes</u> Mr. Kim. ➡ _____

6 The house <u>have</u> a large window. ➡ _____

7 Paul and Liz <u>lives</u> in the city. ➡ _____

B Writing 주어진 말을 이용하여 우리말을 영어로 바꿔 쓰세요.

1 나의 할머니는 꽃을 좋아하신다. (my grandmother, flowers)

➡ My grandmother likes flowers.

2 우리는 주말마다 집을 청소한다. (clean the house, on weekends)

➡ _____

3 Peter는 버스를 운전한다. (drive a bus)

➡ _____

4 그녀는 고양이가 두 마리 있다. (two cats)

➡ _____

5 그 은행은 오후 4시에 문을 닫는다. (the bank, close, at 4:00 p.m.)

➡ _____

C 　내신 대비　질문을 읽고, 알맞은 답을 고르세요.

1 밑줄 친 부분이 올바른 것은?

① Julia studys very hard.

② He always forget his keys.

③ They go to church on Sundays.

④ The boys plays computer games.

2 우리말을 영어로 바르게 옮긴 것은?

> Taylor 선생님은 보통 8시에 학교에 오신다.

① Ms. Taylor usually come to school at 8 o'clock.

② Ms. Taylor come usually to school at 8 o'clock.

③ Ms. Taylor usually comes to school at 8 o'clock.

④ Ms. Taylor comes usually to school at 8 o'clock.

개념 Review

아래 빈칸을 채우면서 개념을 다시 한번 익혀보세요.

❶ 주어 + 일반동사

☑ 일반동사란 go, eat, have 등과 같이 주어의 동작이나 상태를 나타내는 동사예요.

☑ 일반동사 현재형의 긍정문은 주어가 ❶ 　　　　　　　 (he, she, it, 단수 명사)일 때
동사원형 뒤에 -s/es를 붙여요.

❷ 일반동사의 3인칭 단수형

☑ 대부분의 동사 뒤에는 -s를 붙이고, -o, -ch, -sh, -ss, -x로 끝나는 동사 뒤에는 ❷ 　　　　　 를 붙여요.

☑ 「자음＋y」로 끝나는 동사는 y를 ❸ 　　　　　　 로 고치고 -es를 붙여요. 「모음＋y」로 끝나면 -s만 붙여요.

☑ have는 불규칙 동사로 ❹ 　　　　　 로 바꿔요.

UNIT 02 일반동사의 현재형: 부정문 / 의문문

1 부정문

We **don't live** in an apartment.

He **doesn't drink** milk.

주어	don't/doesn't + 동사원형		
I You We They	don't (= do not) 동사원형	I **don't know** you. You **don't live** here. We **don't have** time They **don't watch** TV.	저는 당신을 모릅니다. 너(희)는 여기에 살지 않는다. 우리에게는 시간이 없다. 그들은 TV를 보지 않는다.
He She It	doesn't (= does not)	He **doesn't drive** a car. She **doesn't eat** meat. It **doesn't taste** good.	그는 차를 운전하지 않는다. 그녀는 고기를 먹지 않는다. 그것은 맛이 없다.

☑ 일반동사 현재형의 부정문은 동사 앞에 **don't**(= do not) 또는 **doesn't**(= does not)를 넣어요. 이때 뒤에 오는 동사는 항상 **원형**을 써야 해요. **e.g.** He **doesn't** *drives* a car. (X)

PRACTICE 1 일반동사의 부정문 만들기

① I like sports. → I ____don't____ ____like____ sports.

② She has a dog. → She _____ _____ a dog.

③ We go to school. → We _____ _____ to school.

④ My father wears a tie. → My father _____ _____ a tie.

2 의문문

Do / Does + 주어 + 동사원형 ~?		긍정의 대답	부정의 대답
Do I **know** you? **Do** you **live** here? **Do** we **have** time? **Do** they **watch** TV?	제가 당신을 알고 있나요? 너(희)는 여기에 사니? 우리에게 시간이 있니? 그들은 TV를 보니?	Yes, 주어 + **do**.	No, 주어 + **don't**.
Does he **drive** a car? **Does** she **eat** meat? **Does** it **taste** good?	그는 차를 운전하니? 그녀는 고기를 먹니? 그것은 맛있니?	Yes, 주어 + **does**.	No, 주어 + **doesn't**.

☑ 일반동사 현재형의 의문문은 주어 앞에 **Do** 또는 **Does**를 넣고, 문장 끝에 물음표(?)를 붙여요. 이때 주어 뒤에 오는 동사는 항상 **원형**을 써야 해요. **e.g. Does** she *eats* meat? (X)

PRACTICE 2 일반동사의 의문문 만들기

① You play baseball. ➡ ___Do___ you ___play___ baseball?

② She takes the class. ➡ _____ she _____ the class?

③ Ted walks his dog. ➡ _____ Ted _____ his dog?

④ They need water. ➡ _____ they _____ water?

A ( ) 안에서 알맞은 것을 고르세요.

1 I (don't, doesn't) (like, likes) cheese.

2 She (don't, doesn't) (have, has) much free time.

3 (Do, Does) you (go, goes) to the gym every day?

4 (Do, Does) water (freeze, freezes) at 0°C?

5 The computer (don't, doesn't) (work, works) well.

6 We (don't, doesn't) (want, wants) to go to the party.

7 Steve (don't, doesn't) (live, lives) with his parents.

8 This apple (don't, doesn't) (taste, tastes) good.

9 (Do, Does) they (live, lives) in London?

10 (Do, Does) the bus (run, runs) every ten minutes?

11 He (don't, doesn't) (eat, eats) eggplant.

12 (Do, Does) the baby (cry, cries) often?

13 (Do, Does) all insects (have, has) six legs?

14 Flowers (don't, doesn't) (grow, grows) in winter.

15 (Do, Does) the building (has, have) a parking lot?

 WORDS cheese 치즈   **gym** 체육관, 헬스클럽   **freeze** 얼다, 얼리다   **work** (기계가) 작동되다   **run** 운행하다, 다니다
minute (시간 단위의) 분   **eggplant** 가지   **often** 자주, 종종   **insect** 곤충   **leg** 다리   **grow** 자라다; 재배하다
building 건물   **parking lot** 주차장

B 다음 문장을 ( ) 안의 지시대로 바꿔 쓰세요.

1 You go to school by bus.

(부정문) You ___don't___ ___go___ to school by bus.

(의문문) ___Do___ you ___go___ to school by bus?

2 She has enough money.

(부정문) She _____ _____ enough money.

(의문문) _____ she _____ enough money?

3 He lives in Boston.

(부정문) He _____ _____ in Boston.

(의문문) _____ he _____ in Boston?

4 You know his email address.

(부정문) You _____ _____ his email address.

(의문문) _____ you _____ his email address?

5 They work very hard.

(부정문) They _____ _____ very hard.

(의문문) _____ they _____ very hard?

6 The hotel has a swimming pool.

(부정문) The hotel _____ _____ a swimming pool.

(의문문) _____ the hotel _____ a swimming pool?

7 The book sells well.

(부정문) The book _____ _____ well.

(의문문) _____ the book _____ well?

✏ **WORDS** enough 충분한 address 주소 sell 팔다, 팔리다

영작 술술

A 우리말과 같은 뜻이 되도록 빈칸에 알맞은 말을 쓰세요.

1 너는 K-pop을 좋아하니?

→ ___Do___ ___you___ ___like___ K-pop?

2 그 상점은 과일을 팔지 않는다.

→ The store _____ _____ fruit.

3 그 기차는 30분 후에 떠나니?

→ _____ the train _____ in thirty minutes?

4 그들은 학교까지 걸어가니?

→ _____ they _____ to school?

5 Brian은 오토바이를 타지 않는다.

→ Brian _____ _____ a motorcycle.

6 그녀는 안경을 쓰니?

→ _____ she _____ glasses?

7 Mike와 나는 자주 만나지 않는다.

→ Mike and I _____ _____ very often.

8 나는 피아노를 치지 않는다.

→ I _____ _____ the piano.

9 그 여자아이는 머리가 길지 않다.

→ The girl _____ _____ long hair.

10 너의 엄마는 차를 운전하시니?

→ _____ your mom _____ a car?

Hint

drive	have
leave	like
meet	play
ride	sell
walk	wear

B 주어진 말을 이용하여 우리말을 영어로 바꿔 쓰세요. (부정문은 줄임말로 쓸 것)

1 나에게는 문제가 없다. (a problem)

➡ I don't have a problem.

2 우리는 서로를 모른다. (each other)

➡ _____

3 너는 이탈리아 음식을 좋아하니? (Italian food)

➡ _____

4 그녀는 한국에서 사니? (in Korea)

➡ _____

5 그는 형제가 없다. (a brother)

➡ _____

TIP 1

일반동사의 부정문은 동사 앞에 don't/doesn't를 넣어요. 이때 뒤에 오는 동사는 원형을 써요.

e.g.
- I/You/We/They don't work.
- He/She/It doesn't work.

6 그들은 스키를 즐기지 않는다. (enjoy skiing)

➡ _____

7 너는 펜이 필요하니? (a pen)

➡ _____

8 그 컴퓨터는 잘 작동되지 않는다. (the computer, work well)

➡ _____

TIP 2

일반동사의 의문문은 주어 앞에 Do/Does를 넣어요. 이때 주어 뒤에 오는 동사는 원형을 써요.

e.g.
- Do I/you/we/they work?
- Does he/she/it work?

9 Tom은 한국어를 하니? (speak Korean)

➡ _____

10 그들은 애완동물이 있니? (a pet)

➡ _____

WRAP UP

A Grammar 밑줄 친 부분을 바르게 고쳐 문장을 다시 쓰세요.

1 <u>Are you</u> like classical music? ➡ Do you like classical music?

2 My father <u>don't drive</u> a car. ➡ _____

3 <u>Does she goes</u> to college? ➡ _____

4 Tim <u>doesn't has</u> a bike. ➡ _____

5 <u>Do it</u> smell good? ➡ _____

6 They <u>not do</u> their homework. ➡ _____

7 I <u>am not like</u> onions. ➡ _____

B Writing 주어진 말을 이용하여 우리말을 영어로 바꿔 쓰세요.

1 너는 매일 네 친구들을 만나니? (your friends, every day)

➡ Do you meet your friends every day? _____

2 그녀는 음악을 좋아하니? (music)

➡ _____

3 나는 그의 전화번호를 모른다. (his phone number)

➡ _____

4 그는 라면을 먹지 않는다. (instant noodles)

➡ _____

5 학교 축제는 금요일에 시작합니까? (the school festival, start, on Friday)

➡ _____

C [내신 대비] 질문을 읽고, 알맞은 답을 고르세요.

1   다음 중 틀린 문장은?

   ① Mike don't eat junk food.

   ② Do you go skiing in winter?

   ③ She doesn't care about others.

   ④ Does your father drive to work?

2   다음 문장을 부정문과 의문문으로 바르게 바꾼 것은?

   > She likes action movies.

   ① (부정문) She isn't like action movies.

   (의문문) Is she like action movies?

   ② (부정문) She don't like action movies.

   (의문문) Do she like action movies?

   ③ (부정문) She doesn't like action movies.

   (의문문) Does she like action movies?

   ④ (부정문) She doesn't likes action movies.

   (의문문) Does she likes action movies?

개념 Review

아래 빈칸을 채우면서 개념을 다시 한번 익혀보세요.

❶ 일반동사의 현재형: 부정문

   ☑ 일반동사 현재형의 부정문은 동사 앞에 ❶   또는 ❷   를
   넣어요. 이때 뒤에 오는 동사는 항상 ❸   을 써야 해요.

❷ 일반동사의 현재형: 의문문

   ☑ 일반동사 현재형의 의문문은 주어 앞에 ❹   또는 ❺   를 넣고, 문장 끝에
   물음표(?)를 붙여요. 이때 주어 뒤에 오는 동사는 항상 ❻   을 써야 해요.

01 빈칸에 들어갈 말로 알맞은 것은?

_____ takes the bus to school.

① I
② You
③ The girl
④ Tom and Judy

02 밑줄 친 부분이 틀린 것은?

① My brother likes pizza.
② She washes her hands.
③ The baby crys all the time.
④ Bill does taekwondo very well.

[03-04] 다음 문장을 부정문으로 바르게 바꾼 것을 고르시오.

03

I have a computer in my room.

① I doesn't a computer in my room.
② I have not a computer in my room.
③ I don't have a computer in my room.
④ I'm not have a computer in my room.

04

He checks his email every day.

① He not check his email every day.
② He isn't check his email every day.
③ He don't check his email every day.
④ He doesn't check his email every day.

[05-06] 다음 문장을 의문문으로 바르게 바꾼 것을 고르시오.

05

The kids play on the playground.

① Is the kids play on the playground?
② Do the kids play on the playground?
③ Are the kids play on the playground?
④ Does the kids play on the playground?

06

Jerry spends a lot of time with his family.

① Is Jerry spend a lot of time with his family?
② Do Jerry spends a lot of time with his family?
③ Does Jerry spend a lot of time with his family?
④ Does Jerry spends a lot of time with his family?

07 우리말을 영어로 바르게 옮긴 것은?

그들은 더 이상 여기에 살지 않는다.

① They not live here anymore.
② They don't live here anymore.
③ They aren't live here anymore.
④ They doesn't live here anymore.

08 다음 중 **틀린** 문장은?

① I don't need a new bike.

② Do they live in a big city?

③ Mr. Lee doesn't teach math.

④ Do your father work at a bank?

서술형

[09-11] 주어진 말을 이용하여 우리말을 영어로 바꿔 쓰시오. (부정문은 줄임말로 쓸 것)

09

> 그는 매일 정장을 입는다. (wear, a suit)

➡ _____

10

> 나의 부모님은 스포츠 경기를 즐기지 않으신다.
> (my parents, enjoy, sporting events)

➡ _____

11

> 그녀는 자주 영화를 보러 갑니까?
> (often, go to the movies)

➡ _____

[12-13] 대화의 빈칸에 알맞은 말을 고르시오.

12

> A Kate _____ her jacket with her.
>
> B Really? But it's cold outside.

① don't has

② don't have

③ doesn't has

④ doesn't have

13

> A _____ you know the new English teacher?
>
> B No, I don't.

① Is   ② Are

③ Do   ④ Does

서술형

[14-15] **틀린** 부분을 바르게 고쳐 문장을 다시 쓰시오.

14

> Susan don't watch TV every day.

➡ _____

15

> Does the train arrives on time?

➡ _____

03

현재진행형

학습목표

1 현재진행형의 의미와 현재진행형 동사의 형태를 알아봐요.

2 현재진행형 문장의 부정문과 의문문 만드는 법을 알아봐요.

UNIT 01 현재진행형: 긍정문

1 be동사 + 동사원형-ing

She **is eating** an apple.

They **are doing** the laundry.

주어	am / is / are + 동사원형-ing		
I	am		I **am** read**ing** a book.	나는 책을 읽고 있다.
He She It	is	동사원형-ing	He **is** eat**ing** a snack. She **is** sing**ing** a song. It **is** fly**ing** in the sky.	그는 간식을 먹고 있다. 그녀는 노래를 부르고 있다. 그것은 하늘을 날고 있다.
We You They	are		We **are** plant**ing** trees. You **are** go**ing** to school. They **are** clean**ing** the room.	우리는 나무를 심고 있다. 너(희)는 학교에 가고 있다. 그들은 방을 청소하고 있다.

☑ **현재진행형**은 지금 진행 중인 동작을 나타낼 때 쓰고, 우리말로 '~하고 있다, ~하는 중이다'로 해석해요.

☑ 현재진행형은 「am / is / are + **동사원형-ing**」 형태로 나타내요.

PRACTICE 1 현재진행형 문장 만들기

❶ She wears a mask. → She ____is____ ____wearing____ a mask.

❷ I listen to music. → I _____ _____ to music.

❸ He plays tennis. → He _____ _____ tennis.

❹ We drink juice. → We _____ _____ juice.

2 동사의 -ing형

We **are lying** on snow.

The camel **is sitting**.

동사의 종류	규칙		
대부분의 동사	+-ing	do → doing	work → working
-y로 끝나는 동사	+-ing	buy → buying	study → studying
-e로 끝나는 동사	e를 빼고+-ing	live → living	write → writing
-ie로 끝나는 동사	ie를 y로 고치고+-ing	die → dying	lie → lying
「단모음+단자음」으로 끝나는 동사	자음을 한 번 더 쓰고 +-ing	cut → cutting sit → sitting	run → running swim → swimming

☑ **모음**은 a, e, i, o, u를 가리키고, 모음을 제외한 나머지(b, c, d, f, w, y, z ...)는 **자음**이에요.

☑ **단모음**과 **단자음**은 하나의 모음과 자음을 의미해요.

PRACTICE 2 동사의 -ing형 만들기

① cook ➡ ___cooking___

② read ➡ _____

③ jog ➡ _____

④ sit ➡ _____

⑤ smile ➡ _____

⑥ fly ➡ _____

⑦ lie ➡ _____

⑧ pass ➡ _____

A 주어진 동사를 -ing형으로 바꿔 쓰세요.

1 The girl is ___eating___ ice cream. (eat)

2 Mom is _____ the kitchen. (clean)

3 The boy is _____ a ball. (throw)

4 Mr. Brown is _____ on the chair. (sit)

5 The students are _____ English. (study)

6 Paul is _____ to his friend. (wave)

7 The roses are _____. (die)

8 Many people are _____ for the bus. (wait)

9 I am _____ an email to my friend. (write)

10 Susan is _____ the piano. (play)

11 Mr. and Mrs. Green are _____ TV. (watch)

12 The children are _____ in the lake. (swim)

13 The woman is _____ on the phone. (talk)

14 You are _____ next to the door. (stand)

15 The teachers are _____ a meeting. (have)

 WORDS throw 던지다 sit 앉다 chair 의자 wave (손을) 흔들다 die 죽다 wait for ~을 기다리다 write 쓰다
lake 호수 talk on the phone 통화하다 stand 서다 next to ~의 옆에 have a meeting 회의를 하다

B 다음 문장을 현재진행형으로 바꿔 쓰세요.

1 The phone rings.

→ The phone is ringing.

2 The girl smiles.

→ _____

3 The man works hard.

→ _____

4 You eat a sandwich for lunch.

→ _____

5 Mary buys milk at the supermarket.

→ _____

6 The workers cut the trees.

→ _____

7 He sends an email.

→ _____

8 The dog lies on the floor.

→ _____

9 My brother rides his bicycle.

→ _____

10 The airplane flies above the clouds.

→ _____

 WORDS ring (전화 등이) 울리다   smile 웃다, 미소 짓다   buy 사다   cut 베다, 자르다   send 보내다   lie 눕다
bicycle 자전거   airplane 비행기   above the clouds 구름 위로

A 우리말과 같은 뜻이 되도록 빈칸에 알맞은 말을 쓰세요.

1 Jisu는 영어 시험을 보고 있다.

→ Jisu ___is___ ___taking___ an English exam.

2 엄마는 설거지를 하고 있다.

→ Mom _____ _____ the dishes.

3 Sam과 Emily는 보드 게임을 하고 있다.

→ Sam and Emily _____ _____ a board game.

4 Ken은 그의 의사와 이야기를 하고 있다.

→ Ken _____ _____ to his doctor.

5 그는 자신의 컴퓨터를 사용하고 있다.

→ He _____ _____ his computer.

6 그 학생들은 도서관에서 공부하고 있다.

→ The students _____ _____ at the library.

7 Kate는 인터넷으로 쇼핑을 하고 있다.

→ Kate _____ _____ online.

8 그들은 식당에서 저녁 식사를 하고 있다.

→ They _____ _____ dinner at a restaurant.

Hint

do	have
play	run
shop	study
take	talk
use	wear

9 그 소녀는 그녀의 교복을 입고 있다.

→ The girl _____ _____ her school uniform.

10 Brian은 그의 개와 함께 달리고 있다.

→ Brian _____ _____ with his dog.

B 주어진 말을 이용하여 우리말을 영어로 바꿔 쓰세요.

1   나는 파스타를 먹고 있다. (eat pasta)

➡   I am eating pasta.

2   Susan은 부엌에서 요리를 하고 있다. (cook, in the kitchen)

➡

3   그 소년은 연을 날리고 있다. (the boy, fly a kite)

➡

4   Mike는 통화 중이다. (talk on the phone)

➡

5   우리는 해변에 누워있다. (lie, on the beach)

➡

6   그들은 수영장에서 수영을 하고 있다. (swim, in the pool)

➡

7   Sarah는 선글라스를 쓰고 있다. (wear sunglasses)

➡

8   그는 휴대폰으로 게임을 하고 있다. (play games, on his cellphone)

➡

9   Chris와 나는 숙제를 하고 있다. (do our homework)

➡

10 그들은 휴가를 즐기고 있다. (enjoy their vacation)

➡

TIP 1

현재진행형은 「am/is/
are+동사-ing」형태로
나타내고 '~하고 있다,
~하는 중이다'로 해석해요.

e.g.
- I am eating.
- He is eating.
- You are eating.

TIP 2

동사에 따라 -ing형이
달라져요.

e.g.
- work → working
- make → making
- lie → lying
- run → running

WRAP UP

A Grammar 보기에서 알맞은 말을 골라 현재진행형 문장을 완성하세요.

bake	drink	have	speak	walk	wash

1 Mom _____is_____ _____baking_____ cupcakes.

2 I _____ _____ breakfast.

3 They _____ _____ English.

4 He _____ _____ to school.

5 You _____ _____ orange juice.

6 Kelly _____ _____ her hair.

B Writing 주어진 말을 이용하여 우리말을 영어로 바꿔 쓰세요.

1 Beth는 꽃에 물을 주고 있다. (water the flowers)

➡ ____Beth is watering the flowers.____

2 그들은 잔디밭에 앉아 있다. (sit, on the grass)

➡ _____

3 나는 이를 닦고 있다. (brush my teeth)

➡ _____

4 그녀는 결혼 반지를 끼고 있다. (wear, a wedding ring)

➡ _____

5 Joe는 그의 친구에게 문자를 보내고 있다. (text his friend)

➡ _____

C [내신 대비] 질문을 읽고, 알맞은 답을 고르세요.

1 밑줄 친 부분이 틀린 것은?

① I <u>am taking</u> a shower.

② He <u>is reading</u> a magazine.

③ They <u>are runing</u> in the park.

④ The dog <u>is playing</u> with a ball.

2 우리말을 영어로 바르게 옮긴 것은?

> Jack은 그의 부모님께 편지를 쓰고 있다.

① Jack writes a letter to his parents.

② Jack writing a letter to his parents.

③ Jack is writing a letter to his parents.

④ Jack is writeing a letter to his parents.

개념 Review

아래 빈칸을 채우면서 개념을 다시 한번 익혀보세요.

❶ be동사 + 동사원형-ing

☑ 현재진행형은 지금 진행 중인 동작을 나타낼 때 쓰고, 우리말로 '~하고 있다, ~하는 중이다'로 해석해요.

☑ 현재진행형은 ❶ _____ 형태로 나타내요.

❷ 동사의 -ing형

☑ 모음은 ❷ _____ 를 가리키고, 모음을 제외한 나머지(b, c, d, f, w, y, z ...)는 자음이에요.

☑ ❸ _____ 과 ❹ _____ 은 하나의 모음과 자음을 의미해요.

UNIT 02 현재진행형: 부정문 / 의문문

1 부정문

She **is not doing** her homework.

They **are not playing** soccer.

주어	am / is / are + not + 동사원형-ing		
I	am not		I **am not** walking fast.	나는 빨리 걷고 있지 않다.
He She It	is not	동사원형-ing	He **is not** drinking water. She **is not** watching TV. It **is not** sleeping now.	그는 물을 마시고 있지 않다. 그녀는 TV를 보고 있지 않다. 그것은 지금 자고 있지 않다.
We You They	are not		We **are not** going to the park. You **are not** having lunch. They **are not** learning English.	우리는 공원에 가고 있지 않다. 너(희)는 점심을 먹고 있지 않다. 그들은 영어를 배우고 있지 않다.

☑ 현재진행형의 부정문은 be동사 뒤에 **not**을 붙이면 돼요.

☑ 현재진행형의 부정문은 다음과 같이 줄여 쓸 수 있어요.

   e.g. He **is not** working. = He **isn't** working. / He**'s not** working.

PRACTICE 1   현재진행형 부정문 만들기

❶ They are singing.   ➡   <u>They are not singing.</u>

❷ The baby is crying.   ➡   _____

❸ He is eating pizza.   ➡   _____

❹ We are drawing pictures.   ➡   _____

2 의문문

Am / Is / Are + 주어 + 동사원형-ing ~?		긍정의 대답	부정의 대답
Am I walk**ing** fast?	내가 빨리 걷고 있니?	Yes, you **are**.	No, you **aren't**.
Are you hav**ing** lunch?	너는 점심을 먹고 있니?	Yes, I **am**.	No, I'm **not**.
Is he drink**ing** water?	그는 물을 마시고 있니?	Yes, he **is**.	No, he **isn't**.
Are we go**ing** to the park?	우리는 공원에 가고 있니?	Yes, you **are**.	No, you **aren't**.
Are you hav**ing** lunch?	너희는 점심을 먹고 있니?	Yes, we **are**.	No, we **aren't**.
Are they learn**ing** English?	그들은 영어를 배우고 있니?	Yes, they **are**.	No, they **aren't**.

☑ 현재진행형의 의문문은 주어와 be동사의 순서를 바꾸고, 문장 끝에 물음표(?)를 붙여요.

PRACTICE 2 현재진행형 의문문 만들기

❶ She is opening the door. → ___Is___ she ___opening___ the door?

❷ You are looking at me. → _____ you _____ at me?

❸ He is kicking a ball. → _____ he _____ a ball?

❹ They are jumping rope. → _____ they _____ rope?

A 주어진 말을 이용하여 현재진행형의 부정문 또는 의문문을 완성하세요.

1   ___Is___ he _crossing_ the street? (cross)

2   The worker _____ the roof. (not, fix)

3   _____ she _____ the windows? (clean)

4   I _____ gum. (not, chew)

5   _____ the cat _____ the tree? (climb)

6   _____ Rosa _____ her nails? (bite)

7   They _____ on the bench. (not, sit)

8   _____ David _____ today? (work)

9   She _____ a scarf today. (not, wear)

10   We _____ for an exam. (not, study)

11   Jason _____ in the pool. (not, swim)

12   _____ you _____ of me? (think)

13   _____ the woman _____ the ducks? (feed)

14   Tom and Jane _____ soda. (not, drink)

15   _____ he _____ for the missing key? (look)

WORDS **cross the street** 길을 건너다   **fix** 고치다   **roof** 지붕   **chew** 씹다   **gum** 껌   **climb** 오르다, 등반하다
bite one's nails 손톱을 물어뜯다   **scarf** 스카프, 목도리   **study for an exam** 시험 공부를 하다
think of ~을 생각하다   **feed** 먹이를 주다   **soda** 탄산음료   **look for** ~을 찾다   **missing** 없어진, 실종된

B 다음 문장을 (   ) 안의 지시대로 바꿔 쓰세요.

1 He is playing the guitar.

(부정문) ___He is not playing the guitar.___

(의문문) ___Is he playing the guitar?___

2 The man is fishing in the river.

(부정문) _____

(의문문) _____

3 She is sleeping in her bedroom.

(부정문) _____

(의문문) _____

4 The children are laughing.

(부정문) _____

(의문문) _____

5 Kevin and Cindy are reading comic books.

(부정문) _____

(의문문) _____

6 The cat is chasing the mouse.

(부정문) _____

(의문문) _____

7 Tom is wearing his new T-shirt.

(부정문) _____

(의문문) _____

 WORDS guitar 기타   fish 낚시하다   river 강   laugh (소리 내어) 웃다   comic book 만화책   chase 뒤쫓다
mouse 쥐, 생쥐

영작 술술

A 우리말과 같은 뜻이 되도록 빈칸에 알맞은 말을 쓰세요.

1 그들은 그 호텔에 머물고 있니?

   ➡ _____Are_____ they __staying__ at the hotel?

2 Sally는 라디오를 듣고 있지 않다.

   ➡ Sally _____ _____ _____ to the radio.

3 그들은 해변에 누워 있니?

   ➡ _____ they _____ on the beach?

4 나는 숙제를 하고 있지 않다.

   ➡ I _____ _____ _____ my homework.

5 네 여동생은 모래성을 쌓고 있니?

   ➡ _____ your sister _____ a sandcastle?

6 그 남자는 그의 신발을 신고 있지 않다.

   ➡ The man _____ _____ _____ his shoes.

7 너는 지금 나에게 말하고 있는 거니?

   ➡ _____ you _____ to me now?

8 그들은 우유를 마시고 있지 않다.

   ➡ They _____ _____ _____ milk.

9 그녀는 버스를 기다리고 있니?

   ➡ _____ she _____ for a bus?

10 화재경보기가 울리고 있니?

   ➡ _____ the fire alarm _____?

Hint

build	do
drink	lie
listen	stay
talk	wait
wear	ring

B   주어진 말을 이용하여 우리말을 영어로 바꿔 쓰세요.

1   Ann은 그녀의 어머니를 돕고 있니? (help her mother)

→   Is Ann helping her mother?

2   나는 영어를 공부하고 있지 않다. (study English)

→

3   George는 세차를 하고 있니? (wash his car)

→

4   Olivia는 눈을 감고 있지 않다. (close her eyes)

→

5   그 TV는 지금 작동하지 않는다. (the TV, work, at the moment)

→

6   너는 도서관에 가고 있니? (go to the library)

→

TIP 1

현재진행형의 부정문은
be동사 뒤에 not을 붙여요.

e.g.
- I am not sleeping.
- She is not sleeping.
- They are not sleeping.

7   그들은 중국어를 말하고 있니? (speak Chinese)

→

8   그녀는 전화를 받고 있지 않다. (answer the phone)

→

TIP 2

현재진행형의 의문문은
주어와 be동사의 순서를
바꾸고, 문장 끝에
물음표(?)를 붙여요.

e.g.
- Am I sleeping?
- Is she sleeping?
- Are they sleeping?

9   그 소년들은 집에 오고 있니? (the boys, come home)

→

10   Jimmy는 아무것도 먹고 있지 않다. (eat anything)

→

WRAP UP

A Grammar 밑줄 친 부분을 바르게 고쳐 문장을 다시 쓰세요.

1 I am <u>going not</u> to school. ➡ I am not going to school.

2 The black cat <u>not</u> looking at me. ➡ _____

3 Ann and Mike <u>is</u> not studying. ➡ _____

4 He isn't <u>wear</u> glasses today. ➡ _____

5 <u>Do</u> you carrying a box? ➡ _____

6 Is she <u>make</u> dinner right now? ➡ _____

7 <u>Is</u> the birds drinking water? ➡ _____

B Writing 주어진 말을 이용하여 우리말을 영어로 바꿔 쓰세요.

1 그는 지금 운동하고 있지 않다. (exercise, now)

➡ He is not exercising now.

2 Sue는 피아노를 연습하고 있니? (practice the piano)

➡ _____

3 너는 생일 카드를 쓰고 있니? (write a birthday card)

➡ _____

4 나는 음악을 듣고 있지 않다. (listen to music)

➡ _____

5 그들은 공항에 가고 있니? (go to the airport)

➡ _____

C　내신 대비　질문을 읽고, 알맞은 답을 고르세요.

1 빈칸에 들어갈 말로 알맞은 것은?

> Tom and Sue _____ computer games now.

① don't play

② not playing

③ aren't play

④ aren't playing

2 다음 문장을 의문문으로 바르게 바꾼 것은?

> They are laughing loudly.

① Do they laugh loudly?

② Are they laugh loudly?

③ Do they laughing loudly?

④ Are they laughing loudly?

개념 Review

아래 빈칸을 채우면서 개념을 다시 한번 익혀보세요.

❶ **현재진행형: 부정문**

☑ 현재진행형의 부정문은 be동사 뒤에 ❶ _____ 을 붙이면 돼요.

☑ 현재진행형의 부정문은 다음과 같이 줄여 쓸 수 있어요.

e.g. He is not working. = He ❷ _____ working. / ❸ _____ not working.

❷ **현재진행형: 의문문**

☑ 현재진행형의 의문문은 주어와 ❹ _____ 의 순서를 바꾸고, 문장 끝에 물음표(?)를 붙여요.

01 다음 문장을 아래와 같이 바꿀 때 빈칸에 들어갈 말로 알맞은 것은?

> Bill walks his dog every day.
> → Bill _____ his dog now.

① walks   ② walking

③ is walk   ④ is walking

02 밑줄 친 부분이 올바른 것은?

① Ann is eatting a sandwich.
② Carol is danceing with Bob.
③ The girl is lying on the grass.
④ They are swiming in the pool.

서술형

[03-04] 주어진 단어를 바르게 배열하여 문장을 완성하시오.

03

> working / not / is / the computer / at the moment

➡ _____ .

04

> they / making / are / noise / a lot of

➡ _____ ?

05 빈칸에 들어갈 말이 다른 하나는?

① _____ they playing tennis?

② _____ you listening to music?

③ _____ you watch TV every day?

④ _____ Ben and Susie having lunch?

06 다음 문장을 부정문으로 바르게 바꾼 것은?

> The students are singing together.

① The students not singing together.
② The students do not singing together.
③ The students not are singing together.
④ The students are not singing together.

07 다음 문장을 의문문으로 바르게 바꾼 것은?

> Peter and Julie are holding hands.

① Are Peter and Julie hold hands?
② Is Peter and Julie holding hands?
③ Do Peter and Julie holding hands?
④ Are Peter and Julie holding hands?

[08-09] 우리말을 영어로 바르게 옮긴 것을 고르시오.

08

> 몇몇 새들이 하늘을 날고 있다.

① Some birds fly in the sky.
② Some birds flying in the sky.
③ Some birds are fly in the sky.
④ Some birds are flying in the sky.

09

> Danny가 그의 형과 싸우고 있니?

① Is Danny fight with his brother?
② Is Danny fighting with his brother?
③ Does Danny fight with his brother?
④ Does Danny fighting with his brother?

[10-11] 다음 중 **틀린** 문장을 고르시오.

10 ① Is the rabbit eat a carrot?
② The baby is crying loudly.
③ Are you studying English?
④ She is not talking on the phone.

11 ① Are they sitting on the sofa?
② The cat doesn't sleeping now.
③ Is the man standing on his head?
④ I am hanging a picture on the wall.

[12-13] 대화의 빈칸에 알맞은 말을 고르시오.

12

> A Amy, _____?
> B No, I'm not. I have something
>   in my eye.

① do you cry
② are you cry
③ do you crying
④ are you crying

13

> A What are you doing?
> B _____ dinner for you.

① I make   ② I'm make
③ I'm making   ④ I'm makeing

서술형

[14-15] 주어진 말을 이용하여 우리말을 영어로 바꿔 쓰시오.

14

> 그들은 지하철역으로 걸어가고 있다.
> (walk, to the subway station)

➡ _____

15

> Jessica는 정원에 꽃을 심고 있습니까?
> (plant flowers)

➡ _____
   in the garden?

04

be동사의 과거

학습목표

1 be동사 과거형의 형태를 알아보고, 과거시제와 함께 사용되는 시간 표현을 익혀요.

2 be동사 과거형 문장의 부정문과 의문문 만드는 법을 알아봐요.

UNIT 01 be동사의 과거형: 긍정문

1 was / were

I **was** sick yesterday.

We **were** in science class.

주어	be동사		
I He She It	was	I **was** hungry. He **was** a pilot. She **was** on vacation. It **was** cold this morning.	나는 배가 고팠다. 그는 비행기 조종사였다. 그녀는 휴가 중이었다. 오늘 아침은 추웠다.
We You They	were	We **were** friends. You **were** very brave. They **were** at the mall.	우리는 친구였다. 너(희)는 매우 용감했다. 그들은 쇼핑몰에 있었다.

☑ '~이었다, (~에) 있었다'라고 과거의 상태를 말할 때는 be동사를 **과거형**으로 바꿔주면 돼요. am, is의 과거형은 **was**를, are의 과거형은 **were**를 써요.

PRACTICE 1 was / were 넣기

❶ I _____was_____ at the gym.

❷ It _____ very interesting.

❸ You _____ in the kitchen.

❹ Tom and Jane _____ late for school.

2 과거 시간 표현

She **was** happy **last weekend**.

They **were** in Greece **two weeks ago**.

과거 시간 표현			
yesterday	어제	I was busy **yesterday**.	나는 어제 바빴다.
last week last month last year	지난주 지난달 작년	He was a student **last year**.	그는 작년에 학생이었다.
two days ago three weeks ago five months ago	2일 전 3주 전 5달 전	We were in Paris **two days ago**.	우리는 2일 전에 파리에 있었다.

☑ yesterday, last ~, ~ ago는 과거를 나타내는 시간 표현으로 **과거시제**와 함께 쓰여요.

PRACTICE **2** yesterday / last / ago 넣기

① Bob was 17 years old ____last____ year.

② The weather was good _____ .

③ Jack was absent _____ Monday.

④ My grandparents were young 50 years _____ .

문법 쏙쏙

A ( ) 안에서 알맞은 be동사를 고르세요.

1 I (was, were) in Canada last summer.

2 They (was, were) at work yesterday.

3 The movie (was, were) very boring.

4 The candles (was, were) on the table.

5 My cat (was, were) small five months ago.

6 The teachers (was, were) busy yesterday.

7 Alex (was, were) sick for a week.

8 The doctor (was, were) in his office.

9 Helen and I (was, were) very tired.

10 The windows (was, were) broken.

11 The party last Friday (was, were) fun.

12 The exam (was, were) difficult.

13 Jacob (was, were) born in South Africa.

14 You (was, were) at the concert last night.

15 Picasso (was, were) a great artist.

 **WORDS** boring 지루한   candle 양초   office 사무실   broken 깨진   fun 재미있는, 즐거운   difficult 어려운
be born 태어나다   artist 화가, 예술가

B 다음 문장을 과거시제로 바꿔 쓰세요.

1 The box is empty

→   The box was empty.

2 It is a funny joke.

→

3 Sam and Sarah are my classmates.

→

4 Your name is on the waiting list.

→

5 The clothes are dirty.

→

6 The traffic is heavy.

→

7 Tennis is my favorite sport.

→

8 The car is in the garage.

→

9 My neighbors are kind and friendly.

→

10 Tom and Kate are at my house.

→

 WORDS   empty 비어있는   funny 웃기는, 재미있는   joke 농담   waiting list 대기자 명단   clothes 옷
traffic 교통   garage 차고   neighbor 이웃   friendly 상냥한, 다정한

A 우리말과 같은 뜻이 되도록 빈칸에 알맞은 말을 쓰세요.

1 나는 어제 학교에 늦었다.

→ I ___was___ late for school yesterday.

2 그들은 지난 주말에 부산에 있었다.

→ They _____ in Busan last weekend.

3 우리는 Andy의 집에 있었다.

→ We _____ at Andy's house.

4 Mike는 지난주에 휴가 중이었다.

→ Mike _____ on vacation last week.

5 그 바지는 너무 컸다.

→ The pants _____ too big.

6 그 접시들은 깨끗했다.

→ The dishes _____ clean.

7 그 아이는 이틀 전에 행방불명이었다.

→ The child _____ missing two days ago.

8 Taylor 선생님은 작년에 나의 영어 선생님이었다.

→ Ms. Taylor _____ my English teacher last year.

9 나의 할머니는 1958년에 태어나셨다.

→ My grandmother _____ born in 1958.

10 우리는 어제 해변에 있었다.

→ We _____ at the beach yesterday.

B 주어진 말을 이용하여 우리말을 영어로 바꿔 쓰세요.

1 그 수프는 뜨거웠다. (the soup, hot)

➡ The soup was hot.

2 우리는 어제 놀이공원에 있었다. (at the amusement park)

➡

3 내가 가장 좋아하는 장난감은 테디베어였다. (my favorite toy, a teddy bear)

➡

4 나는 작년에 초등학교에 있었다. (in elementary school)

➡

5 그는 그 동아리의 회원이었다. (a member of the club)

➡

6 우리는 한달 전에 런던에 있었다. (in London, a month)

➡

7 그의 사무실은 7층에 있었다. (his office, on the 7th floor)

➡

8 그것은 멋진 경험이었다. (a wonderful experience)

➡

9 Thomas Edison은 위대한 발명가였다. (a great inventor)

➡

10 그들은 용감한 군인이었다. (brave soldiers)

➡

TIP 1

am과 is의 과거형은 was를, are의 과거형은 were를 써요.

e.g.
- I/He/She/It was
- We/You/They were

TIP 2

yesterday, last ~, ~ ago는 과거를 나타내는 시간 표현으로 과거시제와 함께 쓰여요.

e.g.
- I am sick today.
- I was sick yesterday.

WRAP UP

A Grammar 다음 문장을 과거시제로 바꿔 쓰세요.

1 He is a famous movie star. ➡ He was a famous movie star.

2 The cake is too sweet. ➡ _____

3 They are angry with me. ➡ _____

4 It is a good idea. ➡ _____

5 The rabbits are in the cage. ➡ _____

6 I am at Jane's house. ➡ _____

7 The weather is nice. ➡ _____

B Writing 주어진 말을 이용하여 우리말을 영어로 바꿔 쓰세요.

1 그 문은 어젯밤에 잠겨있었다. (the door, locked)

   ➡ The door was locked last night.

2 그녀는 어제 결석했다. (absent)

   ➡ _____

3 우리는 지난 주말에 집에 있었다. (at home)

   ➡ _____

4 Mark는 3일 전에 아팠다. (sick, days)

   ➡ _____

5 그 해변은 아름다웠다. (the beach, beautiful)

   ➡ _____

C 내신대비 질문을 읽고, 알맞은 답을 고르세요.

1 밑줄 친 부분이 틀린 것은?

① She <u>was</u> born in 1980.

② Cats and dogs <u>are</u> animals.

③ The trees <u>are</u> small last year.

④ Bob <u>was</u> in the hospital three days ago.

2 우리말을 영어로 바르게 옮긴 것은?

> 나의 아파트는 10층에 있었다.

① My apartment is on the 10th floor.

② My apartment are on the 10th floor.

③ My apartment was on the 10th floor.

④ My apartment were on the 10th floor.

개념 Review

아래 빈칸을 채우면서 개념을 다시 한번 익혀보세요.

❶ was / were

☑ '~이었다, (~에) 있었다'라고 과거의 상태를 말할 때는 be동사를 과거형으로 바꿔주면 돼요. am, is의

과거형은 ❶   를, are의 과거형은 ❷   를 써요.

❷ 과거 시간 표현

☑ yesterday, ❸   , ❹   는 과거를 나타내는 시간 표현으로 과거시제와

함께 쓰여요.

UNIT 02 be동사의 과거형: 부정문 / 의문문

1 부정문

He **wasn't** busy last week.

The children **weren't** on the playground.

주어	was / were + not		
I He She It	wasn't (= was not)	I **wasn't** wrong. He **wasn't** a teacher. She **wasn't** tired. It **wasn't** in the car.	나는 틀리지 않았다. 그는 선생님이 아니었다. 그녀는 피곤하지 않았다. 그것은 차 안에 없었다.
We You They	weren't (= were not)	We **weren't** classmates. You **weren't** late for class. They **weren't** at home.	우리는 반 친구가 아니었다. 너(희)는 수업에 늦지 않았다. 그들은 집에 없었다.

☑ be동사 과거형의 부정문은 was, were 뒤에 **not**을 붙이면 돼요.

☑ was not은 **wasn't**로, were not은 **weren't**로 줄여 쓸 수 있어요.

PRACTICE 1 be동사 과거형의 부정문 만들기

❶ I was sad yesterday.   ➡   I wasn't sad yesterday.

❷ We were at the zoo.   ➡   _____

❸ The river was deep.   ➡   _____

❹ The bottles were empty.   ➡   _____

2 의문문

> Were you at school yesterday?

> Yes, I was.

Was / Were＋주어 ~?		긍정의 대답	부정의 대답
Was I wrong?	내가 틀렸었니?		
Was he a teacher?	그는 선생님이었니?	Yes, 주어＋was.	Yes, 주어＋wasn't.
Was she tired?	그녀는 피곤했었니?		
Was it in the car?	그것은 차 안에 있었니?		
Were we classmates?	우리는 반 친구였니?		
Were you late for class?	너(희)는 수업에 늦었니?	Yes, 주어＋were.	Yes, 주어＋weren't.
Were they at home?	그들은 집에 있었니?		

☑ be동사 과거형의 의문문은 현재형과 마찬가지로 주어와 be동사의 순서를 바꾸고, 문장 끝에 물음표(?)를 붙여요.

PRACTICE **2** **be동사 과거형의 의문문 만들기**

❶ You were born in France. → Were you born in France?

❷ He was a good student. → _____

❸ The book was expensive. → _____

❹ They were at work yesterday. → _____

A ( ) 안에서 알맞은 말을 고르세요.

1 I (wasn't, weren't) tired last night.

2 Carol (wasn't, weren't) with us yesterday.

3 My dog (wasn't, weren't) in the park.

4 (Was, Were) they happy at the party?

5 The backpack (wasn't, weren't) very heavy.

6 (Was, Were) you born in Seoul?

7 The cafeteria (wasn't, weren't) clean after lunch.

8 (Was, Were) they on vacation last week?

9 The pizza (wasn't, weren't) delicious.

10 The science class (wasn't, weren't) easy for me.

11 (Was, Were) he the winner of the contest?

12 (Was, Were) they your cousins?

13 Dinner (wasn't, weren't) ready an hour ago.

14 (Was, Were) the children noisy?

15 (Was, Were) your grandmother in the hospital?

WORDS backpack 배낭　cafeteria 카페테리아, 구내식당　delicious 맛있는　winner 우승자　contest 대회, 경연
ready 준비가 된　noisy 시끄러운　in the hospital 입원 중인

B 다음 문장을 (   ) 안의 지시대로 바꿔 쓰세요. (부정문은 줄임말로 쓸 것)

1 The party was fun last weekend.

(부정문) The party wasn't fun last weekend.

(의문문) Was the party fun last weekend?

2 The vase was on the table.

(부정문) _____

(의문문) _____

3 Mike was your best friend.

(부정문) _____

(의문문) _____

4 The car was new.

(부정문) _____

(의문문) _____

5 The people were friendly.

(부정문) _____

(의문문) _____

6 The rumor about him was true.

(부정문) _____

(의문문) _____

7 The shops were open yesterday.

(부정문) _____

(의문문) _____

 WORDS   vase 꽃병   new 새로 산, 새   rumor 소문   true 사실인

A 우리말과 같은 뜻이 되도록 빈칸에 알맞은 말을 쓰세요.

1 그는 네가 좋아하는 가수였니?

➡ __Was__ __he__ your favorite singer?

2 그 신발은 비싸지 않았다.

➡ The shoes _____ _____ expensive.

3 너의 생일은 지난주 금요일이었니?

➡ _____ your birthday last Friday?

4 Jason은 지난주에 휴가 중이었니?

➡ _____ Jason on vacation last week?

5 너의 개는 어젯밤에 아팠니?

➡ _____ your dog sick last night?

6 그 채소들은 신선하지 않았다.

➡ The vegetables _____ _____ fresh.

7 그 우산은 차 안에 없었다.

➡ The umbrella _____ _____ in the car.

8 너는 작년에 6학년이었니?

➡ _____ you in 6th grade last year?

9 그 영화는 재미가 없었다.

➡ The movie _____ _____ interesting.

10 나는 어제 Jane의 집에 없었다.

➡ I _____ _____ at Jane's house yesterday.

B 주어진 말을 이용하여 우리말을 영어로 바꿔 쓰세요. (부정문은 줄임말로 쓸 것)

1 그것은 그의 지갑이 아니었다. (his wallet)

➡ It wasn't his wallet.

2 그 상자들은 충분히 크지 않았다. (the boxes, big enough)

➡

3 그 경기는 흥미진진했니? (the game, exciting)

➡

4 너는 어젯밤에 여기 있었니? (here)

➡

5 그 수업들은 어렵지 않았다. (the classes, difficult)

➡

6 그들은 어제 결석했니? (absent)

➡

7 너는 이 도시에서 태어났니? (born, in this city)

➡

8 어제는 날씨가 추웠니? (the weather, cold)

➡

9 나는 그 시험이 끝난 후 기쁘지 않았다. (happy, after the test)

➡

10 도서관은 어제 문을 열지 않았다. (the library, open)

➡

TIP 1

be동사 과거형의 부정문은 was, were 뒤에 not을 붙이고, 각각 wasn't, weren't로 줄여 쓸 수 있어요.

e.g.
- I / He / She / It
  wasn't[was not]
- We / You / They
  weren't[were not]

TIP 2

be동사 과거형의 의문문은 was, were가 주어 앞에 와요.

e.g.
- Was I / he / she / it ~?
- Were we / you / they ~?

WRAP UP

A Grammar 밑줄 친 부분을 바르게 고쳐 문장을 다시 쓰세요.

1 <u>Was</u> you late for the meeting? ➡ Were you late for the meeting?

2 Jenny <u>were not</u> tired. ➡ _____

3 He <u>be</u> not in class yesterday. ➡ _____

4 We <u>not were</u> sure about it. ➡ _____

5 The weather <u>were not</u> warm. ➡ _____

6 Their car <u>weren't</u> old. ➡ _____

7 <u>Is</u> the movie good last night? ➡ _____

B Writing 주어진 말을 이용하여 우리말을 영어로 바꿔 쓰세요.

1 그것은 좋은 여행이었나요? (a good trip)

➡ Was it a good trip?

2 그 일은 쉽지가 않았다. (the job, easy)

➡ _____

3 그 방은 어둡지 않았다. (the room, dark)

➡ _____

4 그들은 어젯밤에 너무 시끄러웠니? (too noisy)

➡ _____

5 그 의자들은 편안했니? (the chairs, comfortable)

➡ _____

C 내신 대비 질문을 읽고, 알맞은 답을 고르세요.

1 다음 중 틀린 문장은?

① Were the oranges fresh?

② The exam was not difficult.

③ The cat wasn't on the chair.

④ Was the children at the park?

2 다음 문장을 부정문과 의문문으로 바르게 바꾼 것은?

> You were busy yesterday.

① (부정문) You not busy yesterday.

(의문문) You were busy yesterday?

② (부정문) You were not busy yesterday.

(의문문) Were you busy yesterday?

③ (부정문) You was not busy yesterday.

(의문문) Was you busy yesterday?

④ (부정문) You not were busy yesterday.

(의문문) Was you busy yesterday?

개념 Review

아래 빈칸을 채우면서 개념을 다시 한번 익혀보세요.

❶ be동사의 과거형: 부정문

☑ be동사 과거형의 부정문은 was, were 뒤에 ❶   을 붙이면 돼요.

☑ was not은 ❷   로, were not은 ❸   로 줄여 쓸 수 있어요.

❷ be동사의 과거형: 의문문

☑ be동사 과거형의 의문문은 현재형과 마찬가지로 ❹   와 be동사의 순서를 바꾸고, 문장 끝에
물음표(?) 를 붙여요.

01 빈칸에 들어갈 말이 순서대로 바르게 짝지어진 것은?

> Last year, Tim _____ 9 years old.
> Now, he _____ 10 years old.

① is – is
② is – was
③ was – is
④ was – was

02 빈칸에 들어갈 말로 알맞지 않은 것은?

> Mom and Dad were on vacation _____.

① yesterday
② next week
③ last month
④ two days ago

03 다음 문장을 아래와 같이 바꿀 때 빈칸에 알맞은 동사를 쓰시오.

> The children are in the garden now.
> → The children _____ in the garden an hour ago.

[04-05] 우리말을 영어로 바르게 옮긴 것을 고르시오.

04

> Ann과 나는 작년에 5학년이었다.

① Ann and I am in 5th grade last year.
② Ann and I are in 5th grade last year.
③ Ann and I was in 5th grade last year.
④ Ann and I were in 5th grade last year.

05

> 너의 생일 파티는 지난주 금요일이었니?

① Is your birthday party last Friday?
② Are your birthday party last Friday?
③ Was your birthday party last Friday?
④ Were your birthday party last Friday?

[06-07] 다음 문장을 ( ) 안의 지시대로 바꿔 쓰시오.

06

> The cup was broken. (부정문으로)

→ _____

07

> The socks were in the drawer.
> (의문문으로)

→ _____

[08-09] 대화의 빈칸에 알맞은 말을 고르시오.

08

A Were you at home yesterday afternoon?

B No, I _____ at my yoga class.

① is   ② am

③ was   ④ were

09

A Was Peter your classmate?

B Yes, he was. We _____ in the same class.

① is   ② are

③ was   ④ were

서술형

[10-11] 주어진 단어를 바르게 배열하여 문장을 완성하시오.

10

was / my math homework / difficult / not

➡ _____ .

11

loud / was / the music / too

➡ _____ ?

[12-13] 다음 중 **틀린** 문장을 고르시오.

12 ① You were here an hour ago.

② They were on the same team.

③ The man was the winner last year.

④ Kate and her mother was very poor.

13 ① Was the boy in the pool?

② The clothes were not clean.

③ Were your grandmother a teacher?

④ Your parents weren't angry with you.

서술형

[14-15] 주어진 말을 이용하여 우리말을 영어로 바꿔 쓰시오.

14

나는 혼자가 아니었다. (alone)

➡ _____

15

그들은 지난 여름에 유럽에 있었습니까?
(in Europe, summer)

➡ _____

05

일반동사의 과거

학습목표

1 일반동사 과거형의 형태를 알아보고, 불규칙으로 변화하는 동사들을 익혀요.

2 일반동사 과거형 문장의 부정문과 의문문 만드는 법을 알아봐요.

UNIT 01 일반동사의 과거형: 긍정문

1 규칙 동사

We **watched** a movie last night.

My grandmother **hugged** me.

동사의 종류	규칙		
대부분의 동사	+-ed	look → look**ed**	wash → wash**ed**
-e로 끝나는 동사	+-d	dance → dance**d**	smile → smile**d**
「자음+y」로 끝나는 동사	y를 i로 고치고 +-ed	carry → carr**ied**	study → stud**ied**
「모음+y」로 끝나는 동사	+-ed	enjoy → enjoy**ed**	play → play**ed**
「단모음+단자음」으로 끝나는 동사	자음을 한 번 더 쓰고 +-ed	drop → drop**ped** plan → plan**ned**	hug → hug**ged** stop → stop**ped**

☑ 대부분의 일반동사의 과거형은 동사원형에 **-ed**를 붙여 만들어요.

PRACTICE 1 일반동사의 과거형 만들기 (규칙)

1 ask → _____asked_____

2 help → _____

3 close → _____

4 drop → _____

5 cry → _____

6 stay → _____

7 finish → _____

8 plan → _____

2 불규칙 동사

We **made** a snowman yesterday.

He **wrote** a card to his mother.

현재형	과거형	현재형	과거형	현재형	과거형	현재형	과거형
break	**broke**	drive	**drove**	have	**had**	run	**ran**
buy	**bought**	eat	**ate**	make	**made**	say	**said**
come	**came**	get	**got**	meet	**met**	sleep	**slept**
do	**did**	give	**gave**	read	**read**	take	**took**
drink	**drank**	go	**went**	ride	**road**	write	**wrote**

☑ 어떤 동사들은 -ed가 붙어서 과거형이 되지 않고 자신들만의 **불규칙한 과거형**을 갖고 있으므로 잘 외워두어야 해요.
☑ read(읽다, 읽었다), cut(자르다, 잘랐다)처럼 현재형과 과거형의 모양이 같은 동사들도 있어요.

PRACTICE 2 일반동사의 과거형 만들기 (불규칙)

① eat ➡ _____ate_____

② go ➡ _____

③ come ➡ _____

④ do ➡ _____

⑤ run ➡ _____

⑥ sleep ➡ _____

⑦ read ➡ _____

⑧ write ➡ _____

문법 쏙쏙

A 주어진 동사를 과거형으로 바꿔 문장을 완성하세요.

1 Greg __stayed__ at home yesterday. (stay)

2 We _____ for him for 30 minutes. (wait)

3 Dinosaurs _____ many years ago. (live)

4 Jimmy _____ a toy robot for his birthday. (get)

5 The students _____ their final exams. (take)

6 People _____ at the party. (dance)

7 We _____ a wonderful time on our trip. (have)

8 I _____ my arm a month ago. (break)

9 The player _____ the ball. (drop)

10 Tom _____ after the bus. (run)

11 Joe _____ goodbye to his classmates. (say)

12 After lunch, I _____ for an hour. (sleep)

13 Paul _____ his bicycle to school. (ride)

14 Ann _____ a book at the bookstore. (buy)

15 My mom _____ a delicious cake. (make)

WORDS dinosaur 공룡   get 받다   final exams 기말고사   dance 춤추다   break 깨다, 부수다   arm 팔
drop 떨어뜨리다   run after ~을 뒤쫓다   say goodbye 작별 인사를 하다   bookstore 서점

B 다음 문장을 아래와 같이 바꿀 때 빈칸에 알맞은 동사를 쓰세요.

1 I walk to school every day.

→ I ___walked___ to school yesterday.

2 Peter has lunch with his friends every day.

→ Peter _____ lunch with his friends yesterday.

3 They study until 9 o'clock every day.

→ They _____ until 9 o'clock last night.

4 Billy always comes to class late.

→ Billy _____ to class late yesterday.

5 My father and I jog in the park every day.

→ My father and I _____ in the park yesterday.

6 Sarah drinks tea after lunch.

→ Yesterday, Sarah _____ tea after lunch.

7 I do my homework before dinner.

→ I _____ my homework an hour ago.

8 Sam plays computer games every day.

→ Sam _____ computer games yesterday.

9 He reads a book every night.

→ He _____ a book last night.

10 Jane saves 2,000 won every week.

→ Jane _____ 2,000 won last week.

WORDS until ~까지   always 항상   jog 조깅하다   tea 차   save (돈을) 모으다, 저축하다

영작 술술

A 우리말과 같은 뜻이 되도록 빈칸에 알맞은 말을 쓰세요.

1 나는 에어컨을 켰다.

→ I ___turned___ on the air conditioner.

2 Laura는 지난 여름에 밴쿠버에 갔다.

→ Laura _____ to Vancouver last summer.

3 Sam은 어제 집에 페인트 칠을 했다.

→ Sam _____ the house yesterday.

4 우리는 점심으로 피자와 파스타를 먹었다.

→ We _____ pizza and pasta for lunch.

5 아빠는 내 숙제를 도와주셨다.

→ Dad _____ me with my homework.

6 그는 내 생일에 나에게 셔츠 한 벌을 주었다.

→ He _____ me a shirt for my birthday.

7 그들은 이틀 전에 그들의 할아버지를 방문했다.

→ They _____ their grandfather two days ago.

8 우리는 하와이 여행을 즐겼다.

→ We _____ our trip to Hawaii.

9 셰익스피어는 1602년에 〈햄릿〉을 썼다.

→ Shakespeare _____ *Hamlet* in 1602.

10 비는 한 시간 전에 그쳤다.

→ The rain _____ an hour ago.

Hint

eat	enjoy
give	go
help	paint
stop	turn
visit	write

B 주어진 말을 이용하여 우리말을 영어로 바꿔 쓰세요.

1   나는 오늘 아침에 늦게 일어났다. (get up late, this morning)

➡   I got up late this morning.

2   우리는 지난 봄에 캠핑을 갔다. (go camping, spring)

➡   _____

3   Mike는 경주에서 1등을 했다. (come in first in the race)

➡   _____

4   그는 어젯밤에 소파에서 잤다. (sleep, on the sofa)

➡   _____

5   우리는 함께 점심을 먹었다. (have lunch, together)

➡   _____

6   나는 이틀 전에 Susie를 만났다. (meet, days)

➡   _____

TIP 1

대부분의 일반동사는
동사원형에 -ed를 붙여
과거형을 만들어요.

e.g.
- walk → walked
- stay → stayed

7   그들은 공원에서 배드민턴을 쳤다. (play badminton, in the park)

➡   _____

8   그 회의는 11시에 끝났다. (the meeting, end, at 11 o'clock)

➡   _____

TIP 2

불규칙한 과거형을 갖는
동사들은 따로 잘 기억해야
해요.

e.g.
- go → went
- buy → bought
- read → read

9   그는 지난달에 새 차를 샀다. (buy, a new car)

➡   _____

10   그 아기는 한 시간 동안 울었다. (the baby, cry, for an hour)

➡   _____

WRAP UP

A Grammar 밑줄 친 부분을 바르게 고쳐 문장을 다시 쓰세요.

1 She <u>travel</u> to Japan in 2022. ➡ She traveled to Japan in 2022.

2 He <u>works</u> at a bank two years ago. ➡ _____

3 I <u>meeted</u> Jane yesterday. ➡ _____

4 Kim <u>drived</u> to work yesterday. ➡ _____

5 Yesterday, we <u>goed</u> to the zoo. ➡ _____

6 They <u>do</u> a lot of work last week. ➡ _____

7 I <u>runned</u> to school yesterday. ➡ _____

B Writing 주어진 말을 이용하여 우리말을 영어로 바꿔 쓰세요.

1 나는 어젯밤에 축구 경기를 보았다. (watch, a soccer game)

➡ I watched a soccer game last night.

2 John은 오늘 아침에 학교 버스를 놓쳤다. (miss the school bus, this morning)

➡ _____

3 그녀는 지난달에 새 집을 샀다. (buy, a new house)

➡ _____

4 그들은 어제 도서관에서 공부했다. (study, at the library)

➡ _____

5 나는 이 케이크를 혼자서 만들었다. (make this cake, by myself)

➡ _____

C 내신 대비 질문을 읽고, 알맞은 답을 고르세요.

1 다음 동사원형과 과거형이 잘못 짝지어진 것은?

① bake – baked

② stop – stoped

③ carry – carried

④ enjoy – enjoyed

2 빈칸에 들어갈 말로 알맞은 것은?

> John _____ the book five years ago.

① wrote

② writes

③ writed

④ is writing

개념 Review

아래 빈칸을 채우면서 개념을 다시 한번 익혀보세요.

❶ **일반동사의 과거형: 규칙 동사**

☑ 대부분의 일반동사의 과거형은 동사원형에 ❶ _____ 를 붙여 만들어요.

❷ **일반동사의 과거형: 불규칙 동사**

☑ 어떤 동사들은 -ed가 붙어서 과거형이 되지 않고 자신들만의 불규칙한 과거형을 갖고 있으므로 잘 외워

두어야 해요.

☑ ❷ _____ (읽다, 읽었다), ❸ _____ (자르다, 잘랐다)처럼 현재형과 과거형의 모양이

같은 동사들도 있어요.

UNIT 02 일반동사의 과거형: 부정문 / 의문문

1 부정문

I **didn't sleep** well last night.

They **didn't clean** the house.

주어	didn't + 동사원형		
I You We They He She It	didn't (= did not)	동사원형	I **didn't pass** the exam. 나는 시험에 합격하지 않았다. You **didn't meet** Jane. 너(희)는 Jane을 만나지 않았다. We **didn't watch** the movie. 우리는 그 영화를 보지 않았다. They **didn't have** lunch. 그들은 점심을 먹지 않았다. He **didn't study** last night. 그는 어젯밤에 공부하지 않았다. She **didn't buy** a new car. 그녀는 새 차를 사지 않았다. It **didn't arrive** on time. 그것은 제시간에 도착하지 않았다.

☑ 일반동사 과거형의 부정문은 주어에 관계없이 동사 앞에 **didn't**(= **did not**)를 넣어요. 이때 뒤에 오는 동사는 항상 **원형**을 써야 해요. **e.g.** I **didn't** *passed* the exam. (X)

PRACTICE 1   일반동사 과거형의 부정문 만들기

❶ She changed her mind.   → She ___didn't___ ___change___ her mind.

❷ John read my email.   → John _____ _____ my email.

❸ They went to the park.   → They _____ _____ to the park.

❹ I did my homework.   → I _____ _____ my homework.

2 의문문

Did you do your homework?

No, I didn't.

Did+주어+동사원형 ~?		긍정의 대답	부정의 대답
Did I **pass** the exam?	내가 시험에 합격했니?		
Did you **meet** Jane?	너(희)는 Jane을 만났니?		
Did we **watch** the movie?	우리가 그 영화를 봤었니?		
Did they **have** lunch?	그들은 점심을 먹었니?	Yes, 주어+**did**.	No, 주어+**didn't**.
Did he **study** last night?	그녀는 어젯밤에 공부 했니?		
Did she **buy** a new car?	그는 새 차를 샀니?		
Did it **arrive** on time?	그것은 제시간에 도착했니?		

☑ 일반동사 과거형의 의문문은 주어 앞에 **Did**를 넣고, 문장 끝에 물음표(?)를 붙여요. 이때 주어 뒤에 오는 동사는 항상 **원형**을 써야 해요. **e.g. Did** he *studied* last night? (X)

PRACTICE 2 일반동사 과거형의 부정문 만들기

❶ Tom broke the window. → ___Did___ Tom ___break___ the window?

❷ She bought some fruit. → _____ she _____ some fruit?

❸ You went to the dentist. → _____ you _____ to the dentist?

❹ They enjoyed the party. → _____ they _____ the party?

문법 쏙쏙

A 다음 문장을 부정문으로 바꿔 쓰세요. (단, 줄임말로 쓸 것)

1 Ann did the dishes after dinner.

➡ ___Ann didn't do the dishes after dinner.___

2 Sean shaved this morning.

➡ _____

3 We liked the movie.

➡ _____

4 My English improved a lot last year.

➡ _____

5 I emailed my friend yesterday.

➡ _____

6 Sally had the flu last week.

➡ _____

7 My father went to work yesterday.

➡ _____

8 Jerry made his bed this morning.

➡ _____

9 I did my history homework last night.

➡ _____

10 They went on a picnic last weekend.

➡ _____

 WORDS shave 면도하다 **improve** 나아지다, 향상되다 **have the flu** 독감에 걸리다 **go to work** 출근하다
make one's bed 침대를 정돈하다 **history** 역사 **go on a picnic** 소풍을 가다

B 다음 문장을 의문문으로 바꿔 쓰세요.

1 You watched TV last night.

→ _Did you watch TV last night?_

2 Mr. Freeman lived in that house.

→ _____

3 She read my diary.

→ _____

4 They took a lot of photos.

→ _____

5 James ate all the cake.

→ _____

6 You borrowed my pen.

→ _____

7 Mike came home by taxi.

→ _____

8 Your team won the foot volleyball game.

→ _____

9 The teacher erased the board.

→ _____

10 They sold their house.

→ _____

 WORDS diary 일기 take a photo 사진을 찍다 borrow 빌리다 win 이기다 foot volleyball 족구
erase 지우다; 지우개 board 칠판

영작 술술

A 우리말과 같은 뜻이 되도록 빈칸에 알맞은 말을 쓰세요.

1 Tim은 그 셔츠를 사지 않았다.

→ Tim ___didn't___ ___buy___ the shirt.

2 Amy는 송별회에 왔었니?

→ _____ _____ _____ to the farewell party?

3 Clair는 집안일을 끝내지 못했다.

→ Clair _____ _____ the housework.

4 그는 나에게 아무것도 말하지 않았다.

→ He _____ _____ anything to me.

5 너는 어제 인터넷 서핑을 했니?

→ _____ _____ _____ the Internet yesterday?

6 너는 오늘 아침에 꽃에 물을 주었니?

→ _____ _____ _____ the flowers this morning?

7 그들은 지난주 일요일에 수영하러 갔니?

→ _____ _____ _____ swimming last Sunday?

8 그녀는 어제 내 전화를 받지 않았다.

→ She _____ _____ my phone yesterday.

9 너는 그 소식에 대해 들었니?

→ _____ _____ _____ about the news?

10 Mike는 그의 야채들을 먹지 않았다.

→ Mike _____ _____ his vegetables.

Hint

answer	buy
come	eat
finish	go
hear	say
surf	water

B 주어진 말을 이용하여 우리말을 영어로 바꿔 쓰세요. (부정문은 줄임말로 쓸 것)

1 나는 아침 식사를 할 시간이 없었다. (have, time for breakfast)

➡ ___I didn't have time for breakfast.___

2 너는 그 여행이 즐거웠니? (enjoy, the trip)

➡ _____

3 그는 영어를 아주 잘 하지는 못했다. (speak English, very well)

➡ _____

4 그들은 일찍 자러 갔니? (go to bed, early)

➡ _____

5 나는 그의 이름을 기억하지 못했다. (remember, his name)

➡ _____

6 너는 내 문자 메시지를 받았니? (get, my text message)

➡ _____

7 너는 네 이메일을 확인했니? (check, your email)

➡ _____

8 그녀는 자신의 우산을 가져오지 않았다. (bring, her umbrella)

➡ _____

9 너는 파리에서 에펠 탑을 방문했니? (visit, the Eiffel Tower, in Paris)

➡ _____

10 너는 Jane에게 줄 선물을 샀니? (buy, a present, for Jane)

➡ _____

TIP 1

일반동사 과거형의
부정문은 주어에
관계없이 「didn't[did
not]+동사원형」 형태로
써요.

e.g.
- I didn't eat.
- You didn't eat.
- He didn't eat.

TIP 2

일반동사 과거형의
의문문은 「Did+주어+
동사원형 ~?」 형태로 써요.

e.g.
- Did you eat?
- Did they eat?
- Did he eat?

WRAP UP

A   Grammar   주어진 단어를 바르게 배열하여 문장을 완성하세요.

1 (not / did / I / eat)   →   ___I did not eat___   pizza for dinner.

2 (did / go / she)   →   _____ out last night?

3 (he / go / did / not)   →   _____ skiing last winter.

4 (you / did / understand)   →   _____ my question?

5 (they / join / did)   →   _____ the book club?

6 (tell / Tom / didn't)   →   _____ the truth.

7 (did / make / they)   →   _____ the invitation cards?

B   Writing   주어진 말을 이용하여 우리말을 영어로 바꿔 쓰세요.

1 그 소방관은 그 여자아이를 구했나요? (the firefighter, save, the girl)

→   Did the firefighter save the girl? _____

2 그는 어젯밤에 그 문을 잠그지 않았다. (lock, the door)

→ _____

3 너는 네 휴대폰을 껐니? (turn off, your cellphone)

→ _____

4 Sam은 그 문제를 풀지 못했다. (solve, the problem)

→ _____

5 너는 좋은 주말을 보냈니? (have, a good weekend)

→ _____

C 〔내신 대비〕 질문을 읽고, 알맞은 답을 고르세요.

1 다음 중 **틀린** 문장은?

① I didn't think of that.

② Did he read the memo?

③ Did you ate all the cookies?

④ We didn't see him yesterday.

2 다음 문장을 부정문과 의문문으로 바르게 바꾼 것은?

> He bought a new car last month.

① (부정문) He isn't bought a new car last month.

 (의문문) He bought a new car last month?

② (부정문) He wasn't buy a new car last month.

 (의문문) Was he buy a new car last month?

③ (부정문) He didn't buy a new car last month.

 (의문문) Did he buy a new car last month?

④ (부정문) He didn't bought a new car last month.

 (의문문) Did he bought a new car last month?

개념 Review

아래 빈칸을 채우면서 개념을 다시 한번 익혀보세요.

❶ 일반동사의 과거형: 부정문

☑ 일반동사 과거형의 부정문은 주어에 관계없이 동사 앞에 ❶   를 넣어요. 이때 뒤에

오는 동사는 항상 ❷   을 써야 해요.

❷ 일반동사의 과거형: 의문문

☑ 일반동사 과거형의 의문문은 주어 앞에 ❸   를 넣고, 문장 끝에 물음표(?)를 붙여요. 이때

주어 뒤에 오는 동사는 항상 ❹   을 써야 해요.

[01-02] 빈칸에 들어갈 말로 알맞은 것을 고르시오.

01

> Sam _____ to the movies last night.

① go   ② goes
③ went   ④ goed

02

> Mary _____ in Seoul two years ago.

① live   ② lives
③ lived   ④ is living

03 다음 중 동사의 과거형이 <u>잘못</u> 짝지어진 것은?

① eat – ate
② read – read
③ run – runned
④ study – studied

04 밑줄 친 동사를 올바른 형태로 고칠 때 알맞은 것 끼리 짝지어진 것은?

> • The rain <u>stop</u> 30 minutes ago.
> • They <u>come</u> home late last night.

① stops – come
② stoped – came
③ stopped – came
④ stopped – comed

[05-06] 다음 문장을 ( ) 안의 지시대로 바꿔 쓰시오.

05

> John took a taxi to work. (부정문으로)

→ _____

06

> You met the teacher yesterday. (의문문으로)

→ _____

07 빈칸에 들어갈 말이 순서대로 바르게 짝지어진 것은?

> A _____ you do well on the exam?
> B No, I didn't. I _____ many mistakes.

① Do – make
② Did – made
③ Did – maked
④ Were – made

[08-09] 우리말과 같은 뜻이 되도록 주어진 단어를 바르게 배열하시오.

08

> Mina는 2달 전에 그 독서 클럽에 가입했다.
>
> (joined / two months / Mina / ago / the book club.)

➡ _____ .

09

> Olivia는 그녀의 교과서를 수업에 가져오지 않았다.
>
> (bring / Olivia / did / to class / not / her textbooks)

➡ _____ .

[10-11] 밑줄 친 부분이 틀린 것을 고르시오.

10 ① Dad <u>drove</u> to work yesterday.
② I <u>traveled</u> to Italy last summer.
③ They <u>carryed</u> the heavy boxes.
④ We <u>waited</u> for the bus for 30 minutes.

11 ① Tim <u>didn't works</u> last Friday.
② I <u>didn't go</u> to bed early last night.
③ <u>Did you visit</u> your aunt yesterday?
④ <u>Did Mr. Evans come</u> back from vacation?

[12-13] 우리말을 영어로 바르게 옮긴 것을 고르시오.

12

> 나는 점심 식사 후 약을 먹지 않았다.

① I don't take the medicine after lunch.
② I didn't take the medicine after lunch.
③ I didn't took the medicine after lunch.
④ I wasn't take the medicine after lunch.

13

> 그가 이 책을 썼습니까?

① Did he write this book?
② Did he wrote this book?
③ Was he write this book?
④ Does he write this book?

[14-15] 틀린 부분을 바르게 고쳐 문장을 다시 쓰시오.

14

> The movie not did end until midnight.

➡ _____

15

> Do they arrived at the airport on time?

➡ _____

06

미래시제

학습목표

1   will과 be going to를 사용하여 미래의 일을 표현하는 법을 알아봐요.

2   will과 be going to가 쓰인 문장의 부정문과 의문문 만드는 법을 알아봐요.

UNIT 01 will

1 긍정문

The party **will start** soon.

I **will go** to bed early tonight.

주어	will＋동사원형		
I You We They He She It	will (= 'll)	동사원형	I **will go** swimming. 나는 수영하러 갈 것이다. You **will win** the game. 너(희)는 그 경기에서 이길 것이다. We **will play** outside. 우리는 밖에서 놀 것이다. They **will arrive** soon. 그들은 곧 도착할 것이다. He **will cook** dinner. 그가 저녁을 요리할 것이다. She **will visit** the museum. 그녀는 박물관을 방문할 것이다. It **will be** sunny tomorrow. 내일은 맑을 것이다.

☑ '~일 것이다, ~할 것이다'라고 **미래**의 일을 말할 때는 **will**을 써요. 이때 will 뒤에 오는 동사는 항상 **원형**을 써야 해요.

☑ will은 '~할게'라는 **주어의 의지**를 표현하기도 해요. **e.g. Okay, I'll help you.** 좋아, 내가 너를 도와줄게.

PRACTICE 1   **will 문장 만들기**

❶ I go to bed.   →   I ___will___ ___go___ to bed.

❷ He reads the book.   →   He _____ _____ the book.

❸ We take the subway.   →   We _____ _____ the subway.

❹ She opens the door.   →   She _____ _____ the door.

2 부정문 / 의문문

Will Santa come tonight?

Yes, he will.

부정문	I will not go swimming.	나는 수영하러 가지 않을 것이다.
	We will not play outside.	우리는 밖에서 놀지 않을 것이다.
	It won't be sunny tomorrow.	내일은 맑지 않을 것이다.
의문문	A: Will they arrive soon?	그들은 곧 도착할 거니?
	B: Yes, they will. / No, they won't.	응, 그래. / 아니, 그렇지 않아.
	A: Will he cook dinner?	그가 저녁을 요리할 거니?
	B: Yes, he will. / No, he won't.	응, 그래. / 아니, 그렇지 않아.

☑ will의 부정문은 will 뒤에 not을 붙이면 돼요. 이때 will not은 won't로 줄여 쓸 수 있어요.

☑ will의 의문문은 주어와 will의 순서를 바꾸고, 문장 끝에 물음표(?)를 붙여요.

PRACTICE 2 will의 부정문 / 의문문 만들기

① They _____won't_____ _____go_____ to the park. (not, go)

② He _____ _____ us. (not, help)

③ _____ you _____ TV? (watch)

④ _____ they _____ next week? (come)

문법 쏙쏙

A 주어진 말과 will을 이용하여 문장을 완성하세요.

1 (we / go / to the beach / this summer)

➡   We will go to the beach this summer.

2 (the cat / eat / the fish)

➡ _____

3 (they / write / some postcards)

➡ _____

4 (I / order / pizza / for dinner)

➡ _____

5 (the sun / shine / tomorrow)

➡ _____

6 (she / pay / the phone bill / next week)

➡ _____

7 (Susan / wear / that dress / at the wedding)

➡ _____

8 (I / become / a scientist / in the future)

➡ _____

9 (he / keep / his promise)

➡ _____

10 (I / wash / my hair / tonight)

➡ _____

 WORDS postcard 엽서   order 주문하다   shine 빛나다   pay 지불하다   phone bill 전화 요금   dress 드레스, 원피스   wedding 결혼(식)   become ~이 되다   scientist 과학자   in the future 미래에   keep one's promise 약속을 지키다   tonight 오늘 밤

B 빈칸에 will 또는 won't를 넣어 문장을 완성하세요.

1 Don't get up. I ___will___ answer the phone.

2 This shirt is too expensive. I _____ buy it.

3 Sam is a good student. He _____ pass the exam.

4 I'm watching a movie. _____ you be quiet, please?

5 I'm not hungry. I _____ eat the hamburger.

6 John is tired. He _____ stay at home tonight.

7 We are too late. We _____ get there on time.

8 Ethan _____ change his clothes. They are wet.

9 I feel sick. I _____ go to the doctor.

10 _____ robots do housework in the future?

11 You have time. You _____ miss the bus.

12 Don't worry, Peter. I _____ help you.

13 I _____ tell your secret. I promise!

14 Jane sings very well. She _____ become a good singer.

15 Susan is 14 years old. Next year, she _____ be 15.

 WORDS   quiet 조용한   **on time** 정각에, 제시간에   **wet** 젖은   **do housework** 가사일을 하다   **worry** 걱정하다
secret 비밀

A 우리말과 같은 뜻이 되도록 빈칸에 알맞은 말을 쓰세요.

1 그 기차는 곧 도착할 것이다.

→ The train ___will___ ___arrive___ soon.

2 너는 내일 집에 있을 거니?

→ _____ you _____ at home tomorrow?

3 우리는 즐거운 시간을 보낼 것이다.

→ We _____ _____ a great time.

4 그녀는 너의 선물을 좋아할 것이다.

→ She _____ _____ your present.

5 나는 내일부터 조깅을 시작할 것이다.

→ I _____ _____ jogging tomorrow.

6 그는 언젠가 훌륭한 피아니스트가 될 것이다.

→ He _____ _____ a great pianist someday.

7 너는 네 친구들을 초대할 거니?

→ _____ you _____ your friends?

8 내가 문을 열게.

→ I _____ _____ the door.

9 그는 오늘 밤 그 콘서트에 가지 않을 것이다.

→ He _____ _____ to the concert tonight.

10 Tom은 이번 주말에 그의 숙모를 방문하지 않을 것이다.

→ Tom _____ _____ his aunt this weekend.

Hint

arrive	be
become	go
have	like
invite	open
start	visit

B 주어진 말과 will을 이용하여 우리말을 영어로 바꿔 쓰세요.

1 나는 내년에 15살이 될 것이다. (be, 15 years old)

→ I will be 15 years old next year.

2 너는 내일 이 컴퓨터를 쓸 거니? (use, this computer)

→

3 나는 밤에 아무것도 먹지 않을 것이다. (eat, anything, at night)

→

4 날씨가 내일은 흐릴 것이다. (the weather, cloudy)

→

5 내가 나중에 너에게 전화할게. (call you, later)

→

6 나는 네 생일을 잊지 않을게. (forget, your birthday)

→

7 너는 그 시험에 합격할 것이다. (pass the exam)

→

8 Mike가 파티에 올까요? (come to the party)

→

9 그들이 그 아이들을 도와줄까요? (help, the children)

→

10 나는 오늘 저녁에 외출하지 않을 것이다. (go out, this evening)

→

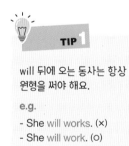

TIP 1

will 뒤에 오는 동사는 항상 원형을 써야 해요.

e.g.
- She will works. (x)
- She will work. (o)

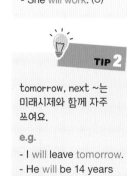

TIP 2

tomorrow, next ~는 미래시제와 함께 자주 쓰여요.

e.g.
- I will leave tomorrow.
- He will be 14 years old next year.

WRAP UP

A Grammar 다음 문장을 will을 사용하여 미래시제로 바꿔 쓰세요.

1 He fixes the car. → _He will fix the car._

2 The dog does not bite you. → _____

3 Do you go to the movies? → _____

4 I read the magazine. → _____

5 Does she listen to music? → _____

6 They build a new house. → _____

7 We are not at school. → _____

B Writing 주어진 말과 will을 이용하여 우리말을 영어로 바꿔 쓰세요.

1 나는 언젠가 그를 만날 것이다. (meet him, someday)

→ _I will meet him someday._

2 John은 내일 집에 없을 것이다. (at home)

→ _____

3 그 시험은 쉽지 않을 것이다. (the exam, easy)

→ _____

4 그가 10시에는 돌아올까요? (come back, at 10 o'clock)

→ _____

5 네가 오늘 밤 저녁을 요리할 거니? (cook dinner, tonight)

→ _____

C [내신 대비] 질문을 읽고, 알맞은 답을 고르세요.

1 다음 중 올바른 문장은?

① She wills visit her grandparents.

② My sister won't ate the spinach.

③ He will learn to swim this summer.

④ Will you are at home for Christmas?

2 우리말을 영어로 바르게 옮긴 것은?

> 너는 내일 치과에 갈거니?

① Do you go to the dentist tomorrow?

② Are you go to the dentist tomorrow?

③ Will you go to the dentist tomorrow?

④ Will you going to the dentist tomorrow?

개념 Review

아래 빈칸을 채우면서 개념을 다시 한번 익혀보세요.

❶ will: 긍정문

☑ '~일 것이다, ~할 것이다'라고 미래의 일을 말할 때는 ❶ _____ 을 써요. 이때 will 뒤에 오는

동사는 항상 ❷ _____ 을 써야 해요.

❷ will: 부정문 / 의문문

☑ will의 부정문은 will 뒤에 ❸ _____ 을 붙이면 돼요. 이때 will not은 ❹ _____ 로 줄여

쓸 수 있어요.

☑ will의 의문문은 ❺ _____ 와 will의 순서를 바꾸고, 문장 끝에 물음표(?)를 붙여요.

UNIT 02 be going to

1 긍정문

I **am going to travel** in July.

We **are going to move** tomorrow.

주어	be going to + 동사원형		
I	am going to		I **am going to meet** my friend. 나는 내 친구를 만날 것이다.
He She It	is going to	동사원형	He **is going to study** tonight. 그는 오늘밤 공부할 것이다.
We You They	are going to		They **are going to go** fishing. 그들은 낚시하러 갈 것이다.

☑ '~일 것이다, ~할 것이다'라고 **미래의 일**을 말할 때는 will 대신 **be going to**를 쓸 수도 있어요.

☑ '~할 예정이다'라고 **미리 예정된 계획**을 말할 때도 be going to를 사용해요.

PRACTICE 1 be going to 문장 만들기

❶ I take a shower. → I ___am___ going to ___take___ a shower.

❷ He learns Spanish. → He _____ going to _____ Spanish.

❸ We buy groceries. → We _____ going to _____ groceries.

❹ They finish school. → They _____ going to _____ school.

2 부정문 / 의문문

부정문	I **am not going to meet** my friend. He **is not going to study** tonight. They **are not going to go** fishing.	나는 내 친구를 만나지 않을 것이다. 그는 오늘밤 공부하지 않을 것이다. 그들은 낚시하러 가지 않을 것이다.
의문문	A: **Is he going to study** tonight? B: Yes, he **is.** / No, he **isn't.** A: **Are** they **going to go** fishing? B: Yes, they **are.** / No, they **aren't.**	그는 오늘밤 공부할 거니? 응, 그래. / 아니, 그렇지 않아. 그들은 낚시하러 가지 않을 것이다. 응, 그래. / 아니, 그렇지 않아.

☑ be going to의 부정문은 be동사 뒤에 **not**을 붙여서 만들어요.
☑ be going to의 의문문은 주어와 be동사의 순서를 바꾸고, 문장 끝에 물음표(?)를 붙여요.

PRACTICE **2** **be going to의 부정문 / 의문문 만들기**

① I _____am not going to walk_____ to school today. (not, walk)

② They _____ in the tent. (not, sleep)

③ _____ you _____? (sing)

④ _____ she _____ a cake? (make)

문법 쏙쏙

A 다음 문장을 be going to를 사용하여 바꿔 쓰세요.

1   He will watch a movie tonight.

→   He is going to watch a movie tonight.

2   They will wait at the park.

→ _____

3   Jack will play the drums in the band.

→ _____

4   We will sell the furniture.

→ _____

5   I will buy a new smartphone.

→ _____

6   They will travel abroad this year.

→ _____

7   Fred will walk to the station.

→ _____

8   My parents will meet my teacher.

→ _____

9   The groom will sing a song for the bride.

→ _____

10 Jane and I will go shopping this afternoon.

→ _____

WORDS   drum 북, 드럼   band 밴드, 악단   furniture 가구   abroad 해외로   station 역   groom 신랑
bride 신부   go shopping 쇼핑하러 가다

B 다음 문장을 ( ) 안의 지시대로 바꿔 쓰세요.

1 She is going to do the work.

(부정문)   She is not going to do the work.

(의문문)   Is she going to do the work?

2 You are going to wash the jeans.

(부정문)

(의문문)

3 The man is going to be in trouble.

(부정문)

(의문문)

4 We are going to miss our plane.

(부정문)

(의문문)

5 The movie is going to start on time.

(부정문)

(의문문)

6 The police are going to catch the thief.

(부정문)

(의문문)

7 The bridge is going to fall down.

(부정문)

(의문문)

 WORDS   jeans 청바지   be in trouble 곤경에 처하다   police 경찰   catch 붙잡다   thief 도둑   bridge 다리
fall down 무너지다

A 우리말과 같은 뜻이 되도록 빈칸에 알맞은 말을 쓰세요.

1 너는 TV를 볼 거니?

→ ____Are____ you going to __watch__ TV?

2 그 축구 경기는 흥미진진할 것이다.

→ The soccer game _____ going to _____ exciting.

3 그녀는 약속을 지키지 않을 것이다.

→ She _____ _____ going to _____ her promise.

4 Janet은 오늘 저녁에 요리를 하지 않을 것이다.

→ Janet _____ _____ going to _____ this evening.

5 나는 생일 파티를 열지 않을 것이다.

→ I _____ _____ going to _____ a birthday party.

6 우리는 그것에 대해 더 이상 이야기하지 않을 것이다.

→ We _____ _____ going to _____ about it anymore.

7 우리는 이번 주 토요일에 박물관에 갈 것이다.

→ We _____ going to _____ to the museum this Saturday.

8 그들은 버스 정류장까지 걸어갈 거니?

→ _____ they going to _____ to the bus stop?

9 그는 우리를 돕지 않을 것이다.

→ He _____ _____ going to _____ us.

10 네가 그 개에게 먹이를 줄 거니?

→ _____ you going to _____ the dog?

Hint	
be	cook
feed	go
have	keep
help	talk
walk	watch

B 주어진 말과 be going to를 이용하여 우리말을 영어로 바꿔 쓰세요.

1 우리는 다음 주에 바쁠 것이다. (busy)

→   We are going to be busy next week.

2 그는 그 모자를 사지 않을 것이다. (buy, the hat)

→ _____

3 너는 내일 떠날 예정이니? (leave)

→ _____

4 우리는 늦지 않을 것이다. (late)

→ _____

5 그들은 그 기차를 탈 거니? (take the train)

→ _____

6 그가 나에게 편지를 보낼까요? (send me a letter)

→ _____

7 Sarah는 다음 달에 이사를 할 것이다. (move)

→ _____

8 우리는 집을 청소할 거니? (clean the house)

→ _____

9 Steve는 그의 직장을 그만둘 것이다. (quit his job)

→ _____

10 나는 다음 달에 유럽을 여행할 것이다. (travel to Europe)

→ _____

TIP 1

미래의 일에 대한 예측이나 미리 예정된 계획은 「be going to＋동사원형」으로 나타내요.

e.g.
- I am going to leave.
- He is going to leave.
- They are going to leave.

TIP 2

버스, 택시, 지하철 등의 교통수단을 '타다, 이용하다'라고 할 때는 동사 take를 사용해요.

e.g.
- take the bus
- take the a taxi
- take the subway

WRAP UP

A Grammar 다음 문장을 be going to를 사용하여 미래시제로 바꿔 쓰세요.

1 Carol visits her aunt. ➡ Carol is going to visit her aunt.

2 I don't practice the piano. ➡ _____

3 He gets a new job. ➡ _____

4 Do you meet him? ➡ _____

5 Does she make bread? ➡ _____

6 We don't take a vacation. ➡ _____

7 Are they busy? ➡ _____

B Writing 주어진 말과 be going to를 이용하여 우리말을 영어로 바꿔 쓰세요.

1 우리는 재미있게 보낼 것이다. (have fun)

➡ We are going to have fun.

2 그는 머리를 자를 것이다. (get a haircut)

➡ _____

3 그녀가 나에게 전화를 할까요? (call me)

➡ _____

4 나는 그를 기다리지 않을 것이다. (wait for him)

➡ _____

5 너는 방과 후에 숙제를 할 거니? (do your homework, after school)

➡ _____

C 내신대비 질문을 읽고, 알맞은 답을 고르세요.

1 밑줄 친 부분의 의미가 <u>다른</u> 하나는?

① Is she <u>going</u> to feed the cat?

② Are you <u>going</u> to get a puppy?

③ I am <u>going</u> to meet Ann at 6:00.

④ We are <u>going</u> to the station now.

2 다음 문장을 부정문과 의문문으로 바르게 바꾼 것은?

> The baby is going to take a nap.

① (부정문) The baby is going not to take a nap.

(의문문) Is the baby going to take a nap?

② (부정문) The baby is not going to take a nap.

(의문문) Is the baby going to take a nap?

③ (부정문) The baby is not going to take a nap.

(의문문) Does the baby going to take a nap?

④ (부정문) The baby won't going to take a nap.

(의문문) Will the baby going to take a nap?

개념 Review

아래 빈칸을 채우면서 개념을 다시 한번 익혀보세요.

❶ **be going to: 긍정문**

☑ '~일 것이다, ~할 것이다'라고 미래의 일을 말할 때는 will 대신 ❶   를 쓸 수도 있어요.

☑ '~할 예정이다'라고 미리 예정된 ❷   을 말할 때도 be going to를 사용해요.

❷ **be going to: 부정문 / 의문문**

☑ be going to의 부정문은 be동사 뒤에 ❸   을 붙여서 만들어요.

☑ be going to의 의문문은 주어와 ❹   의 순서를 바꾸고, 문장 끝에 물음표(?)를 붙여요.

[01-02] 대화의 빈칸에 알맞은 말을 고르시오.

01

> A This box is too heavy.
> B Okay, I _____ it for you.

① carry

② carried

③ will carry

④ am carrying

04 두 문장이 같은 뜻이 되도록 할 때 빈칸에 알맞은 말은?

> Will you buy a new computer?
> → _____ buy a new computer?

① Do you

② Are you go to

③ Are you going to

④ Will you going to

05 빈칸에 들어갈 말로 알맞지 <u>않은</u> 것은?

> We are going to watch a movie _____.

① tonight

② yesterday

③ tomorrow

④ next week

02

> A We _____ get married on July 2.
> B Congratulations!

① is going to

② am going to

③ are going to

④ will going to

06 짝지어진 문장의 의미가 서로 <u>다른</u> 것은?

① I will meet my friends.

  = I am going to meet my friends.

② They will leave tomorrow.

  = They are going to leave tomorrow.

③ We will travel by bus.

  = We are going to travel by bus.

④ The children will go to the zoo.

  = The children are going to the zoo.

서술형

03 다음 문장을 아래와 같이 바꿀 때 빈칸에 알맞은 동사를 쓰시오.

> It is cold this winter.
> → It will _____ cold this winter.

서술형

[07-08] 우리말과 같은 뜻이 되도록 주어진 단어를 바르게 배열하시오.

07

John은 곧 새 직장을 구할 것이다.

(get / John / will / a new job)

➜ _____ soon.

08

Sally는 일요일에 테니스를 치지 않을 것이다.

(tennis / is / to / Sally / not / play / going)

➜ _____

on Sunday.

[09-10] 우리말을 영어로 바르게 옮긴 것을 고르시오.

09

Mike는 그 경기에서 우승하지 않을 것이다.

① Mike won't win the game.
② Mike not will win the game.
③ Mike does not win the game.
④ Mike will not winning the game.

10

너는 내일 Peter를 초대할 거니?

① Do you invite Peter tomorrow?
② Do you go to invite Peter tomorrow?
③ Are you go to invite Peter tomorrow?
④ Are you going to invite Peter tomorrow?

[11-12] 다음 중 <u>틀린</u> 문장을 고르시오.

11 ① Will they like the idea?
② I will learn to play the guitar.
③ He will be not at home tonight.
④ Will she come to the party next week?

12 ① I am going to take the next bus.
② Is she going to reads the book?
③ We are going to have lunch at noon.
④ Mom is not going to buy any sweets.

서술형

[13-15] 주어진 말을 이용하여 우리말을 영어로 바꿔 쓰시오.

13

나는 그의 충고를 받아들일 것이다.

(will, take his advice)

➜ _____

14

그 시험은 어렵지 않을 것이다.

(the test, be going to, difficult)

➜ _____

15

내일은 날씨가 좋을까요?

(the weather, be going to, good)

➜ _____

Grammar +Plus Writing

START

WORKBOOK

1

DARAKWON

Grammar +Plus Writing

START

WORKBOOK 1

be동사의 현재형: 긍정문

A 밑줄 친 부분이 맞으면 O를 쓰고, **틀리면** 바르게 고치세요.

1 Mary <u>am</u> a doctor. ➡ _____

2 You <u>is</u> very smart. ➡ _____

3 Seoul <u>are</u> a big city. ➡ _____

4 The cats <u>is</u> small. ➡ _____

5 Mr. Smith <u>is</u> very kind. ➡ _____

6 Lisa <u>am</u> my sister. ➡ _____

7 Jack and Lucy <u>is</u> in the classroom. ➡ _____

8 <u>She're</u> at the library. ➡ _____

9 Mark <u>is</u> strong. ➡ _____

10 They <u>is</u> actors. ➡ _____

11 Your brother <u>are</u> tall. ➡ _____

12 Ben <u>is</u> my best friend. ➡ _____

13 The bag <u>are</u> full. ➡ _____

14 <u>They's</u> happy. ➡ _____

15 We <u>am</u> at the bus stop. ➡ _____

Chapter 01

Answer Key p.22

B   주어진 말을 이용하여 우리말을 영어로 바꿔 쓰세요.

1   우리는 학생이다. (students)

➡ _____

2   나는 11살이다. (11 years old)

➡ _____

3   Luis는 멕시코 출신이다. (from Mexico)

➡ _____

4   그 책들은 내 가방에 있다. (the books, in my bag)

➡ _____

5   그것은 내가 가장 좋아하는 음식이다. (my favorite food)

➡ _____

6   마드리드는 스페인에 있다. (Madrid, in Spain)

➡ _____

7   너는 좋은 친구야. (a good friend)

➡ _____

8   그의 고양이는 주황색이다. (his cat, orange)

➡ _____

9   돌고래들은 영리하다. (dolphins, clever)

➡ _____

10   Daniel과 나는 영화관에 있다. (at the movie theater)

➡ _____

A 다음 문장을 ( ) 안의 지시대로 바꿔 쓰세요.

1 You are cold. (의문문)

➡ _____

2 I am a teacher. (부정문)

➡ _____

3 Pablo is my friend. (부정문)

➡ _____

4 He is a fast runner. (의문문)

➡ _____

5 You are late. (부정문)

➡ _____

6 The pen is red. (의문문)

➡ _____

7 They are interested in art. (의문문)

➡ _____

8 Our dog is sick. (부정문)

➡ _____

9 Your parents are at home. (의문문)

➡ _____

10 The cat is under the bed. (부정문)

➡ _____

B 주어진 말을 바르게 배열하여 문장을 완성하세요.

1 그는 프랑스인이 아니다. (French, not, he, is)

➡ _____

2 Abby는 내 여동생이 아니다. (is, my sister, not, Abby)

➡ _____

3 그들은 서울에 없다. (in Seoul, they, not, are)

➡ _____

4 그것은 식탁 위에 없다. (it, not, on the table, is)

➡ _____

5 나는 요리를 잘 못한다. (am, good at, I, not, cooking)

➡ _____

6 너는 목이 마르니? (you, thirsty, are)

➡ _____

7 Anna는 너의 반 친구니? (your classmate, Anna, is)

➡ _____

8 그 바지는 너무 크니? (are, too big, the pants)

➡ _____

9 우리는 학교에 늦었니? (school, are, late for, we)

➡ _____

10 너는 어둠을 무서워하니? (you, the dark, are, afraid of)

➡ _____

일반동사의 현재형: 긍정문

A 밑줄 친 부분이 맞으면 O를 쓰고, 틀리면 바르게 고치세요.

1   They <u>play</u> soccer on weekends.   ➡ _____

2   She <u>have</u> breakfast every morning.   ➡ _____

3   Oliver <u>brush</u> his teeth before bed.   ➡ _____

4   My brother <u>exercise</u> every day.   ➡ _____

5   My parents <u>watch</u> TV after work.   ➡ _____

6   Harper <u>study</u> English at school.   ➡ _____

7   The owl <u>sleep</u> in a tree.   ➡ _____

8   I <u>drink</u> orange juice in the morning.   ➡ _____

9   Ava <u>sing</u> beautifully.   ➡ _____

10   John and Linda <u>take</u> a walk in the park.   ➡ _____

11   We <u>visit</u> our grandparents on Sundays.   ➡ _____

12   The bakery <u>open</u> at 10:00 a.m.   ➡ _____

13   Ms. Johnson often <u>stay</u> up late.   ➡ _____

14   Joe <u>listen</u> to music in the car.   ➡ _____

15   My sister <u>do</u> yoga every morning.   ➡ _____

Answer Key p.22

B 주어진 말을 이용하여 우리말을 영어로 바꿔 쓰세요.

1 나는 아이스크림을 좋아한다. (like, ice cream)

   ➡ _____

2 Debby는 흰색 고양이 한 마리가 있다. (have, a white cat)

   ➡ _____

3 우리는 함께 저녁을 요리한다. (cook dinner, together)

   ➡ _____

4 그 드론은 하늘 높이 난다. (the drone, fly, high in the sky)

   ➡ _____

5 Sarah는 주말마다 쇼핑을 하러 간다. (go shopping, on weekends)

   ➡ _____

6 그는 학교에서 영어를 가르친다. (teach English, at school)

   ➡ _____

7 Peter는 매일 그의 개를 산책시킨다. (walk his dog, every day)

   ➡ _____

8 그 소녀는 피아노를 매우 잘 친다. (the girl, play the piano, very well)

   ➡ _____

9 그는 파란색 차를 운전한다. (drive, a blue car)

   ➡ _____

10 그들은 매주 일요일에 집을 청소한다. (clean the house, every Sunday)

   ➡ _____

일반동사의 현재형: 부정문 / 의문문

A 다음 문장을 ( ) 안의 지시대로 바꿔 쓰세요. (부정문은 줄임말로 쓸 것)

1 My cat likes water. (부정문)

➡ _____

2 My cousins live in New York. (부정문)

➡ _____

3 He speaks Chinese. (의문문)

➡ _____

4 Steve plays the guitar. (의문문)

➡ _____

5 The house has a garden. (부정문)

➡ _____

6 They work in this building. (의문문)

➡ _____

7 My mother drinks coffee. (부정문)

➡ _____

8 I watch TV in the morning. (부정문)

➡ _____

9 Mark goes to the gym every day. (의문문)

➡ _____

10 You listen to the radio. (의문문)

➡ _____

Answer Key p.23

B 우리말을 참고하여 밑줄 친 부분을 바르게 고쳐 문장을 다시 쓰세요.

1 I <u>not like</u> spicy food.   나는 매운 음식을 좋아하지 않는다.

   ➡ _____

2 He <u>don't have</u> a smartphone.   그는 스마트폰이 없다.

   ➡ _____

3 <u>Does Sue dances</u> ballet well?   Sue는 발레를 잘 추니?

   ➡ _____

4 <u>Do it rain</u> a lot here?   여기는 비가 많이 오니?

   ➡ _____

5 Chris <u>don't work</u> on weekends.   Chris는 주말에는 일하지 않는다.

   ➡ _____

6 My parents <u>travel not</u> often.   나의 부모님은 자주 여행을 하시지는 않는다.

   ➡ _____

7 <u>Does your friends use</u> social media?   너의 친구들은 소셜 미디어를 사용하니?

   ➡ _____

8 She <u>don't watches</u> horror movies.   그녀는 공포 영화를 보지 않는다.

   ➡ _____

9 <u>Do they studies</u> hard for their exams? 그들은 시험을 위해 열심히 공부하니?

   ➡ _____

10 <u>Do you and Kelly goes</u> to the same school? 너와 Kelly는 같은 학교에 다니니?

   ➡ _____

현재진행형: 긍정문

A 주어진 동사를 현재진행형으로 바꿔 문장을 완성하세요.

1 I _____ _____ milk. (drink)

2 It _____ _____ outside. (rain)

3 The sun _____ _____ brightly. (shine)

4 The boys _____ _____ in the race. (run)

5 John _____ _____ down the street. (walk)

6 The man _____ _____ a bicycle. (ride)

7 We _____ _____ for the exam. (study)

8 Eric _____ _____ in the park. (jog)

9 They _____ _____ at the hotel. (stay)

10 The flowers _____ _____. (die)

11 Rosa _____ _____ her name. (write)

12 I _____ _____ vegetables. (cut)

13 Jack and Jill _____ _____ in the yard. (play)

14 The soccer player _____ _____ a ball. (kick)

15 They _____ _____ in the sea. (swim)

Answer Key p.23

B **주어진 말을 이용하여 우리말을 영어로 바꿔 쓰세요.**

1 나는 지금 아침 식사를 하고 있다. (have breakfast, now)

➡ _____

2 그들은 집에서 영화를 보고 있다. (watch a movie, at home)

➡ _____

3 그녀는 지금 책을 읽고 있다. (read a book, now)

➡ _____

4 Sarah는 숙제를 하고 있다. (do her homework)

➡ _____

5 그들은 케이크를 만들고 있다. (make a cake)

➡ _____

6 우리는 식료품을 사고 있다. (buy groceries)

➡ _____

7 그는 킥보드를 타고 있다. (ride a scooter)

➡ _____

8 그 개는 햇볕에 누워 있다. (the dog, lie, in the sun)

➡ _____

9 그는 마라톤을 하고 있다. (run a marathon)

➡ _____

10 그 사람들은 바닥에 앉아 있다. (the people, sit on the floor)

➡ _____

현재진행형: 부정문 / 의문문

A 다음 문장을 (   ) 안의 지시대로 바꿔 쓰세요.

1 It is snowing outside. (부정문)

➡ _____

2 He is running to school. (의문문)

➡ _____

3 The dog is barking loudly. (부정문)

➡ _____

4 We are watching the news. (부정문)

➡ _____

5 She is painting a picture. (의문문)

➡ _____

6 I am exercising at the gym. (부정문)

➡ _____

7 You are shopping at the mall. (의문문)

➡ _____

8 Rick and Mary are talking on the phone. (의문문)

➡ _____

9 They are dancing at the party. (부정문)

➡ _____

10 I am looking good today. (의문문)

➡ _____

Answer Key p.23

B 주어진 말을 바르게 배열하여 문장을 완성하세요.

1 우리는 해변에 가고 있지 않다. (not, are, we, going, to the beach)

➡ _____

2 Anna는 버스를 기다리고 있지 않다. (the bus, Anna, not, is, waiting for)

➡ _____

3 그 소들은 풀을 먹고 있지 않다. (eating, not, the cows, are, grass)

➡ _____

4 나는 이를 닦고 있지 않다. (brushing, I, not, my teeth, am)

➡ _____

5 엄마와 아빠는 웃고 있지 않다. (are, Mom and Dad, not, laughing)

➡ _____

6 그 앵무새는 말하고 있니? (the parrot, talking, is)

➡ _____

7 그 아이들은 게임을 하고 있니? (playing, the children, games, are)

➡ _____

8 Peter는 상자를 들고 있니? (Peter, carrying, is, a box)

➡ _____

9 Alice는 새 드레스를 입고 있니? (is, a new dress, Alice, wearing)

➡ _____

10 너는 계단을 내려가고 있니? (you, walking, are, down the stairs)

➡ _____

be동사의 과거형: 긍정문

A 빈칸에 was, were 중 알맞은 것을 쓰세요.

1 I _____ at school at 9 o'clock yesterday.

2 My grandmother _____ a teacher ten years ago.

3 The soccer players _____ thirsty after the game.

4 Mr. White _____ in the hospital last week.

5 It _____ cold and windy yesterday.

6 My sister _____ in elementary school last year.

7 Ryan and Lucy _____ 12 years old last year.

8 The watermelon _____ sweet and juicy.

9 You _____ at the zoo last Friday.

10 Marie Curie _____ a great scientist.

11 They _____ classmates in high school.

12 We _____ the champions last year.

13 They _____ my neighbors five years ago.

14 The book _____ in my bag this morning.

15 My parents _____ in the living room an hour ago.

Answer Key p.23

B 주어진 말을 이용하여 우리말을 영어로 바꿔 쓰세요.

1 그들은 지난 여름에 파리에 있었다. (in Paris, summer)

   ➡ _____

2 그녀는 나의 엄마의 가장 친한 친구였다. (my mom's best friend)

   ➡ _____

3 그 케이크는 맛있었다. (the cake, delicious)

   ➡ _____

4 그는 작년에 나의 수학 선생님이었다. (my math teacher)

   ➡ _____

5 베토벤은 위대한 작곡가였다. (Beethoven, a great composer)

   ➡ _____

6 우리는 2주 전에 휴가 중이었다. (on vacation, weeks)

   ➡ _____

7 Jane과 Mike는 지난주 일요일에 쇼핑몰에 있었다. (at the mall, Sunday)

   ➡ _____

8 나는 오늘 아침에 학교에 늦었다. (late for school, this morning)

   ➡ _____

9 나의 부모님은 어제 바쁘셨다. (my parents, busy)

   ➡ _____

10 그 아이들은 도서관에서 조용했다. (the children, quiet, in the library)

   ➡ _____

be동사의 과거형: 부정문 / 의문문

A 다음 문장을 ( ) 안의 지시대로 바꿔 쓰세요. (부정문은 줄임말로 쓸 것)

1 The school trip was enjoyable. (부정문)

➡ _____

2 We were happy after the game. (부정문)

➡ _____

3 It was good news. (의문문)

➡ _____

4 Mr. Smith was a good teacher. (의문문)

➡ _____

5 She was at the party last night. (부정문)

➡ _____

6 He was interested in the book. (부정문)

➡ _____

7 You were at home all day yesterday. (의문문)

➡ _____

8 The pants were on sale. (의문문)

➡ _____

9 They were in the office on Friday. (부정문)

➡ _____

10 The gloves were in your coat pockets. (의문문)

➡ _____

Answer Key p.24

B **주어진 말을 이용하여 우리말을 영어로 바꿔 쓰세요. (부정문은 줄임말로 쓸 것)**

1 그 영화는 별로 무섭지 않았다. (the movie, very scary)

→ _____

2 그녀는 작년에 교사가 아니었다. (a teacher)

→ _____

3 그 펜들은 필통에 없었다. (the pens, in the pencil case)

→ _____

4 나는 오늘 아침에 피곤하지 않았다. (tired, this morning)

→ _____

5 그 식당은 어제 붐비지 않았다. (the restaurant, crowded)

→ _____

6 그 수업은 너무 어려웠니? (the lesson, too difficult)

→ _____

7 그 가게는 지난주 월요일에 문을 열었니? (the store, open, Monday)

→ _____

8 그들은 그 결과에 만족했니? (happy with the results)

→ _____

9 그 책은 재미있었니? (the book, interesting)

→ _____

10 너는 10분 전에 여기에 있었니? (here, 10 minutes)

→ _____

일반동사의 과거형: 긍정문

A 주어진 동사를 과거형으로 바꿔 문장을 완성하세요.

1 We _____ the sunset yesterday. (watch)

2 The cat _____ off the table. (jump)

3 They _____ together at the party. (dance)

4 She _____ heavy groceries to her house. (carry)

5 He _____ a colorful picture. (paint)

6 We _____ a surprise party for Anna's birthday. (plan)

7 Mr. Davis _____ at the gas station. (stop)

8 They _____ the concert last night. (enjoy)

9 Judy _____ her favorite mug this morning. (break)

10 I _____ a picture with a famous actor. (take)

11 Joe _____ his friends to the airport. (drive)

12 She _____ lemonade on a hot day. (drink)

13 I _____ a fresh sandwich for lunch. (eat)

14 Jake _____ his bike to his friend's house. (ride)

15 She _____ a letter to her best friend. (write)

Chapter 05

Answer Key p.24

B 주어진 말을 이용하여 우리말을 영어로 바꿔 쓰세요.

1 그 소녀는 나를 보고 미소를 지었다. (the girl, smile at me)

➡ _____

2 Isabel은 그 공연에서 피아노를 연주했다. (play the piano, at the concert)

➡ _____

3 그는 두 시간 동안 영어를 공부했다. (study English, for two hours)

➡ _____

4 나의 엄마는 나를 꼭 안아주셨다. (hug me, tightly)

➡ _____

5 우리는 해변에 수영을 하러 갔다. (go swimming, at the beach)

➡ _____

6 Pedro는 지난주에 새 스마트폰을 샀다. (buy, a new smartphone)

➡ _____

7 그들은 어젯밤에 텐트에서 잤다. (sleep in a tent)

➡ _____

8 나는 어제 만화책 몇 권을 읽었다. (read some comic books)

➡ _____

9 그는 자신의 친구들에게 작별 인사를 했다. (say goodbye, to his friends)

➡ _____

10 그 학생들은 버스에서 내렸다. (the students, get off the bus)

➡ _____

UNIT 02 일반동사의 과거형: 부정문 / 의문문

A 다음 문장을 ( ) 안의 지시대로 바꿔 쓰세요. (부정문은 줄임말로 쓸 것)

1 We went to the beach yesterday. (부정문)

→ _____

2 Mr. Brown drank coffee. (의문문)

→ _____

3 I met Louis at the restaurant. (부정문)

→ _____

4 They did the laundry yesterday. (부정문)

→ _____

5 He moved to San Francisco. (의문문)

→ _____

6 Emma quit her job last week. (의문문)

→ _____

7 We ate ice cream for dessert. (부정문)

→ _____

8 Jeff rode the roller coaster. (의문문)

→ _____

9 I bought onions at the supermarket. (부정문)

→ _____

10 She won first prize at the contest. (의문문)

→ _____

B 주어진 말을 바르게 배열하여 문장을 완성하세요.

1 Nick은 새 노트북을 사지 않았다. (didn't, Nick, a new laptop, buy)

   ➡ _____

2 그 아기는 낮잠을 자지 않았다. (the baby, take, didn't, a nap)

   ➡ _____

3 나는 오늘 아침에 피곤하지 않았다. (tired, feel, I, this morning, didn't)

   ➡ _____

4 그는 자신의 지갑을 가져오지 않았다. (bring, didn't, he, his wallet)

   ➡ _____

5 그녀는 내게 아무 말도 하지 않았다. (say, she, anything, didn't, to me)

   ➡ _____

6 Carol은 감기에 걸렸니? (Carol, a cold, catch, did)

   ➡ _____

7 Hans는 그의 친구와 싸웠니? (fight, did, with his friend, Hans)

   ➡ _____

8 너는 네 숙제를 했니? (did, do, you, your homework)

   ➡ _____

9 그들은 영국에서 자랐니? (grow up, they, did, in England)

   ➡ _____

10 그 수업은 9시 30분에 시작했니? (the class, start, did, at 9:30)

   ➡ _____

UNIT 01 will

A 주어진 말과 will을 이용하여 문장을 완성하세요.

1 I _____ you at 2 o'clock. (meet)

2 I feel hungry. I _____ some snacks. (eat)

3 David _____ his dog for a walk. (take)

4 Hurry up. The bus _____ for us. (not, wait)

5 _____ a scientist in the future? (you, become)

6 _____ lunch at the cafeteria? (they, have)

7 It _____ tomorrow. It will be sunny. (not, rain)

8 _____ the next game? (you, play)

9 The dinner _____ ready in 5 minutes. (be)

10 Jim is angry with me. He _____ to me. (not, talk)

11 Take this medicine. You _____ much better. (feel)

12 I am too tired. I _____ out tonight. (not, go)

13 _____ the computer for her report? (she, use)

14 _____ on the moon someday? (people, live)

15 The movie is scary. I _____ it. (not, watch)

Answer Key p.25

B 주어진 말을 바르게 배열하여 문장을 완성하세요.

1   그들은 내년 봄에 꽃을 심을 것이다. (plant, next spring, they, flowers, will)

➡ _____

2   Betty는 다음 주에 바쁠 것이다. (be, next week, Betty, busy, will)

➡ _____

3   우리는 공항까지 택시로 갈 것이다. (go to, will, by taxi, we, the airport)

➡ _____

4   나는 내 친구의 숙제를 도와줄 것이다. (help, will, my friend, I, with his homework)

➡ _____

5   우리는 월요일에 시험을 보지 않을 것이다. (we, a test, won't, on Monday, have)

➡ _____

6   나는 다음 주말에 너를 방문할 것이다. (next weekend, I, will, you, visit)

➡ _____

7   그들은 내일 집에 없을 것이다. (won't, tomorrow, be, they, at home)

➡ _____

8   그 콘서트는 곧 시작하니? (the concert, soon, will, start)

➡ _____

9   너는 토요일에 결혼식에 갈 거니? (to the wedding, will, on Saturday, you, go)

➡ _____

10   Mary는 내년에 대학을 졸업하니? (Mary, graduate from, will, college, next year)

➡ _____

be going to

A 다음 문장을 be going to를 사용하여 바꿔 쓰세요.

1 I will go to the dentist tomorrow.

→ _____

2 Mr. Green will teach us next semester.

→ _____

3 Bob and Kate will see a movie tonight.

→ _____

4 My brother will take his driving test tomorrow.

→ _____

5 She won't buy that expensive dress.

→ _____

6 We won't see each other for a while.

→ _____

7 They won't travel abroad this summer.

→ _____

8 Will you go shopping tomorrow?

→ _____

9 Will he be late for the meeting?

→ _____

10 Will they get married soon?

→ _____

Answer Key p.25

B 우리말을 참고하여 밑줄 친 부분을 바르게 고쳐 문장을 다시 쓰세요.

1 The plane going to take off in half an hour. 그 비행기는 30분 후에 이륙할 예정이다.

→ _____

2 Her baby will going to be born in July. 그녀의 아기는 7월에 태어날 예정이다.

→ _____

3 He is going work in Japan for a year. 그는 일 년 동안 일본에서 일할 것이다.

→ _____

4 Alex and Mia is going to paint the room. Alex와 Mia는 그 방을 페인트칠할 것이다.

→ _____

5 Eric is going not to go surfing tomorrow. Eric은 내일 서핑하러 가지 않을 것이다.

→ _____

6 I am not go to watch TV tonight. 나는 오늘 밤에 TV를 보지 않을 것이다.

→ _____

7 We will not going to play tennis today. 우리는 오늘 테니스를 치지 않을 것이다.

→ _____

8 Is the train will going to arrive soon? 기차가 곧 도착할 예정이니?

→ _____

9 Are they go to move to a bigger house? 그들은 더 큰 집으로 이사할 거니?

→ _____

10 Does he going to buy a new scooter? 그는 새 킥보드를 살 거니?

→ _____

Chapter 01

UNIT 01 be동사의 현재형: 긍정문

단어	뜻	단어 쓰기	뜻 쓰기
01 classroom	명 교실		
02 glad	형 기쁜		
03 city	명 도시		
04 interesting	형 재미있는		
05 mistake	명 실수		
06 sick	형 아픈		
07 notebook	명 노트, 공책		
08 uncle	명 삼촌		
09 angry	형 화난		
10 aunt	명 숙모, 고모, 이모		
11 dirty	형 더러운, 지저분한		
12 classmate	명 급우, 반 친구		
13 tall	형 키가 큰		
14 favorite	형 좋아하는		
15 twin	명 쌍둥이		
16 tired	형 피곤한		
17 expensive	형 비싼		
18 dentist	명 치과 의사		

단어		뜻	단어 쓰기	뜻 쓰기
19	floor	명 층, 바닥		
20	famous	형 유명한 be famous for ~로 유명하다		
21	musician	명 음악가		
22	season	명 계절		
23	handsome	형 잘생긴		
24	puppy	명 강아지		
25	sleepy	형 졸린		
26	pilot	명 비행기 조종사		
27	clever	형 영리한		
28	scary	형 무서운		
29	cousin	명 사촌		
30	brave	형 용감한		

UNIT 02 be동사의 현재형: 부정문 / 의문문

단어		뜻	단어 쓰기	뜻 쓰기
01	late	형 늦은 부 늦게		
02	actor	명 배우		
03	lazy	형 게으른		
04	kitchen	명 부엌, 주방		
05	nurse	명 간호사		
06	thirsty	형 목마른		
07	library	명 도서관		

08	question	명 질문, 문재	
09	people	명 사람들	
10	be afraid of	~을 두려워[무서워]하다	
11	snake	명 뱀	
12	be interested in	~에 관심[흥미]이 있다	
13	bright	형 밝은	
14	birthday	명 생일	
15	vegetable	명 야채, 채소	
16	refrigerator	명 냉장고	
17	post office	명 우체국	
18	fault	명 잘못	
19	right	형 옳은, 맞는	
20	wrong	형 틀린	
21	free	형 한가한 명 자유	
22	strict	형 엄격한	
23	liar	명 거짓말쟁이	
24	married	형 결혼한	
25	heavy	형 무거운	
26	children	명 아이들 child 아이, 어린이	
27	fat	형 뚱뚱한	
28	light	형 가벼운	
29	alone	형 혼자	
30	museum	명 박물관	

Chapter 02

다음 단어들을 잘 듣고 따라 쓴 후 그 뜻을 쓰세요.

UNIT 01 일반동사의 현재형: 긍정문

단어	뜻	단어 쓰기	뜻 쓰기
01 live	동 살다		
02 speak	동 말하다		
03 glasses	명 안경		
04 breakfast	명 아침 식사		
05 drive	동 운전하다		
06 bone	명 뼈		
07 walk	명 걷기, 산책 동 걷다 go for a walk 산책하러 가다		
08 lunch	명 점심 식사		
09 beautiful	형 아름다운		
10 town	명 마을, 소도시		
11 leave	동 떠나다		
12 cost	동 (비용이) ~이다		
13 forget	동 잊다, 잊어버리다		
14 exercise	동 운동하다		
15 church	명 교회 go to church 교회에 가다		
16 enjoy	동 즐기다		
17 homework	명 숙제		
18 cry	동 울다		

19	help	동 돕다	
20	voice	명 목소리	
21	brush	동 닦다 brush one's teeth 이를 닦다	
22	twice	명 두 번 twice a day 하루에 두 번	
23	drink	동 마시다	
24	usually	부 보통, 평소에	
25	stay	동 머무르다, 있다	
26	weekend	명 주말	
27	meet	동 만나다	
28	listen to	~을 듣다	
29	early	부 일찍	
30	skip	동 거르다, 빼먹다	

UNIT 02 일반동사의 현재형: 부정문 / 의문문

단어		뜻	단어 쓰기	뜻 쓰기
01	know	동 알다, 알고 있다		
02	meat	명 고기		
03	taste	동 ~ 맛이 나다		
04	baseball	명 야구 play baseball 야구를 하다		
05	cheese	명 치즈		
06	gym	명 체육관, 헬스클럽		
07	freeze	동 얼다, 얼리다		

08	work	동 일하다; (기계가) 작동되다
09	run	동 달리다; 운행하다, 다니다
10	minute	명 (시간 단위의) 분
11	eggplant	명 가지
12	often	부 자주, 종종
13	insect	명 곤충
14	leg	명 다리
15	grow	동 자라다; 재배하다
16	building	명 건물
17	parking lot	명 주차장
18	enough	형 충분한 부 충분히
19	address	명 주소
20	sell	동 팔다, 팔리다
21	fruit	명 과일
22	ride	동 타다
23	motorcycle	명 오토바이
24	problem	명 문제
25	each other	서로
26	pet	명 애완동물
27	college	명 대학
28	smell	동 ~ 냄새가 나다
29	onion	명 양파
30	festival	명 축제

Chapter 03

다음 단어들을 잘 듣고 따라 쓴 후 그 뜻을 쓰세요.

UNIT 01 현재진행형: 긍정문

단어	뜻	단어 쓰기	뜻 쓰기
01 plant	동 심다		
02 throw	동 던지다		
03 sit	동 앉다		
04 chair	명 의자		
05 wave	동 (손을) 흔들다		
06 die	동 죽다		
07 wait for	~을 기다리다		
08 write	동 쓰다		
09 lake	명 호수		
10 stand	동 서다		
11 next to	전 ~의 옆에		
12 ring	동 (전화 등이) 울리다 / 명 반지		
13 smile	동 웃다, 미소 짓다		
14 buy	동 사다		
15 cut	동 베다, 자르다		
16 send	동 보내다		
17 lie	동 눕다, 누워 있다		
18 bicycle	명 자전거		

19	airplane	명 비행기
20	exam	명 시험 take an exam 시험을 보다
21	dish	명 접시 do the dishes 설거지를 하다
22	dinner	명 저녁 식사
23	restaurant	명 식당
24	school uniform	명 교복
25	kite	명 연 fly a kite 연을 날리다
26	beach	명 해변
27	vacation	명 휴가, 방학 on vacation 휴가 중인
28	bake	동 굽다
29	water	명 물 동 물을 주다
30	grass	명 풀, 잔디밭

UNIT 02 현재진행형: 부정문 / 의문문

단어	뜻	단어 쓰기	뜻 쓰기
01 learn	동 배우다		
02 draw	동 그리다		
03 look at	~을 보다		
04 kick	동 (발로) 차다		
05 jump rope	줄넘기를 하다		
06 cross	동 건너다 cross the street 길을 건너다		
07 fix	동 고치다		

08	roof	몡 지붕		
09	chew	동 씹다		
10	climb	동 오르다, 등반하다		
11	bite	동 물다 bite one's nails 손톱을 물어뜯다		
12	scarf	몡 스카프, 목도리		
13	feed	동 먹이를 주다		
14	look for	~을 찾다		
15	missing	형 없어진, 실종된		
16	guitar	몡 기타 play the guitar 기타를 치다		
17	fish	동 낚시하다 몡 물고기, 생선		
18	river	몡 강		
19	laugh	동 (소리 내어) 웃다		
20	chase	동 뒤쫓다		
21	mouse	몡 쥐, 생쥐		
22	build	동 짓다, 세우다		
23	sandcastle	몡 모래성 build a sandcastle 모래성을 쌓다		
24	eye	몡 눈		
25	moment	몡 순간 at the moment 지금		
26	answer	동 대답하다, (전화를) 받다		
27	carry	동 들다, 나르다		
28	practice	동 연습하다		
29	airport	몡 공항		
30	loudly	부 큰 소리로		

Chapter 04 다음 단어들을 잘 듣고 따라 쓴 후 그 뜻을 쓰세요.

 be동사의 과거형: 긍정문

단어	뜻	단어 쓰기	뜻 쓰기
01 **yesterday**	명 어제		
02 **last**	형 지난		
03 **ago**	부 ~ 전에		
04 **weather**	명 날씨		
05 **absent**	형 결석한		
06 **grandparents**	명 조부모님		
07 **young**	형 젊은, 어린		
08 **boring**	형 지루한		
09 **candle**	명 양초		
10 **office**	명 사무실		
11 **broken**	형 깨진		
12 **fun**	형 재미있는, 즐거운		
13 **difficult**	형 어려운		
14 **be born**	태어나다		
15 **artist**	명 화가, 예술가		
16 **empty**	형 비어 있는		
17 **funny**	형 웃기는, 재미있는		
18 **joke**	명 농담		

단어	뜻	단어 쓰기	뜻 쓰기
19 clothes	명 옷		
20 traffic	명 교통		
21 garage	명 차고		
22 neighbor	명 이웃		
23 friendly	형 상냥한, 다정한		
24 amusement park	명 놀이공원		
25 elementary school	명 초등학교		
26 wonderful	형 멋진		
27 experience	명 경험		
28 inventor	명 발명가		
29 soldier	명 군인		
30 cage	명 우리, 새장		

UNIT 02 be동사의 과거형: 부정문 / 의문문

단어	뜻	단어 쓰기	뜻 쓰기
01 deep	형 깊은		
02 bottle	명 병		
03 backpack	명 배낭		
04 cafeteria	명 카페테리아, 구내식당		
05 delicious	형 맛있는		
06 winner	명 우승자		
07 contest	명 대회, 경연		

08	ready	형 준비가 된
09	noisy	형 시끄러운
10	hospital	명 병원 in the hospital 입원 중인
11	vase	명 꽃병
12	new	형 새로 산, 새
13	rumor	명 소문
14	true	형 사실인
15	fresh	형 신선한
16	umbrella	명 우산
17	grade	명 학년
18	wallet	명 지갑
19	game	명 게임, 경기
20	exciting	형 신나는, 흥미진진한
21	sure	형 확신하는
22	warm	형 따뜻한
23	old	형 오래된
24	trip	명 여행
25	job	명 일, 직장
26	dark	형 어두운
27	comfortable	형 편안한
28	socks	명 양말
29	drawer	명 서랍
30	poor	형 가난한

UNIT 01 일반동사의 과거형: 긍정문

단어	뜻	단어 쓰기	뜻 쓰기
01 hug	동 껴안다		
02 snowman	명 눈사람		
03 dinosaur	명 공룡		
04 get	동 받다, 얻다		
05 dance	동 춤추다		
06 break	동 깨다, 부수다		
07 arm	명 팔		
08 drop	동 떨어뜨리다		
09 goodbye	명 작별 인사 say goodbye 작별 인사를 하다		
10 bookstore	명 서점		
11 until	전 ~까지		
12 always	부 항상		
13 jog	동 조깅하다		
14 tea	명 차		
15 save	동 저축하다; 구하다		
16 turn on	켜다		
17 air conditioner	명 에어컨		
18 paint	동 페인트를 칠하다; 그리다		

19	give	동 주다		
20	shirt	명 셔츠		
21	visit	동 방문하다		
22	rain	명 비 동 비가 오다		
23	stop	동 멈추다		
24	camping	명 캠핑, 야영 go camping 캠핑을 가다		
25	spring	명 봄		
26	race	명 경주		
27	badminton	명 배드민턴 play badminton 배드민턴을 치다		
28	end	동 끝나다		
29	travel	동 여행하다 travel to ~로 여행하다		
30	miss	동 놓치다; 그리워하다		

UNIT 02 일반동사의 과거형: 부정문 / 의문문

	단어	뜻	단어 쓰기	뜻 쓰기
01	pass	동 합격하다, 통과하다		
02	arrive	동 도착하다		
03	change	동 바꾸다		
04	mind	명 마음		
05	shave	동 면도하다		
06	improve	동 나아지다, 향상되다		
07	flu	명 독감		

08	history	몡 역사		
09	picnic	몡 소풍 go on a picnic 소풍을 가다		
10	diary	몡 일기		
11	photo	몡 사진 take a photo 사진을 찍다		
12	borrow	동 빌리다		
13	win	동 이기다		
14	erase	동 지우다 몡 지우개		
15	board	몡 칠판		
16	finish	동 끝내다		
17	housework	몡 가사일		
18	surf	동 인터넷을 서핑[검색]하다		
19	news	몡 뉴스, 소식		
20	remember	동 기억하다		
21	bring	동 가져오다		
22	present	몡 선물		
23	understand	동 이해하다		
24	join	동 가입하다		
25	truth	몡 진실		
26	invitation	몡 초대, 초대장		
27	firefighter	몡 소방관		
28	lock	동 잠그다		
29	turn off	~을 끄다		
30	solve	동 (문제를) 풀다, 해결하다		

 **Chapter 06**

다음 단어들을 잘 듣고 따라 쓴 후 그 뜻을 쓰세요.

 **UNIT 01** will

단어	뜻	단어 쓰기	뜻 쓰기
01 **soon**	부 곧		
02 **outside**	부 밖에, 밖에서		
03 **sunny**	형 화창한, 맑은		
04 **tomorrow**	명 내일		
05 **subway**	명 지하철		
06 **next**	형 다음의		
07 **postcard**	명 엽서		
08 **order**	동 주문하다		
09 **shine**	동 빛나다		
10 **pay**	동 지불하다		
11 **bill**	명 고지서, 청구서		
12 **dress**	명 드레스, 원피스		
13 **wedding**	명 결혼(식)		
14 **become**	동 ~이 되다		
15 **scientist**	명 과학자		
16 **future**	명 미래 in the future 미래에		
17 **promise**	명 약속 동 약속하다		
18 **tonight**	명 오늘 밤		

19	quiet	형 조용한		
20	wet	형 젖은		
21	worry	동 걱정하다		
22	secret	명 비밀		
23	start	동 시작하다		
24	great	형 훌륭한		
25	pianist	명 피아니스트		
26	someday	부 언젠가		
27	invite	동 초대하다		
28	cloudy	형 흐린		
29	call	동 전화하다		
30	spinach	명 시금치		

UNIT 02 be going to

단어		뜻	단어 쓰기	뜻 쓰기
01	shower	명 샤워 take a shower 샤워를 하다		
02	grocery	명 식료품 buy groceries 식료품을 사다		
03	Spanish	명 스페인어　형 스페인의		
04	tent	명 텐트		
05	drum	명 북, 드럼 play the drums 드럼을 연주하다		
06	band	명 밴드, 악단		
07	furniture	명 가구		

08	abroad	🔵부 해외로
09	station	🔵명 역
10	groom	🔵명 신랑
11	bride	🔵명 신부
12	shopping	🔵명 쇼핑 go shopping 쇼핑하러 가다
13	jeans	🔵명 청바지
14	trouble	🔵명 곤경, 문제 be in trouble 곤경에 처하다
15	police	🔵명 경찰
16	catch	🔵동 붙잡다
17	thief	🔵명 도둑
18	bridge	🔵명 다리
19	talk	🔵동 말하다, 이야기하다
20	anymore	🔵부 더 이상
21	bus stop	🔵명 버스 정류장
22	hat	🔵명 모자
23	letter	🔵명 편지
24	move	🔵동 이사하다
25	quit	🔵동 그만두다
26	bread	🔵명 빵
27	haircut	🔵명 이발, 머리 깎기 get a haircut 머리를 자르다
28	nap	🔵명 낮잠 take a nap 낮잠을 자다
29	noon	🔵명 정오, 낮 12시 at noon 정오에
30	advice	🔵명 충고, 조언

Grammar Plus Writing

START

Grammar Plus Writing

START

ANSWER KEY

1

DARAKWON

Grammar +Plus Writing

START

ANSWER KEY 1

UNIT **01** be동사의 현재형: 긍정문

PRACTICE **1**
p.10

1 is	**2** is	**3** are
4 are	**5** am	**6** are
7 is	**8** are	

해설

be동사의 현재형은 주어에 따라 am, is, are를 쓴다. 주어가 I이면 am을, you나 복수 주어이면 are를 쓴다. '나(I)'와 '너(you)'를 뺀 나머지 단수 주어(He, Jane, The dog)에는 is를 쓴다.

PRACTICE **2**
p.11

1 She's	**2** It's
3 You're	**4** I'm

해설

인칭대명사와 be동사는 아포스트로피(')를 사용해 줄여 쓸 수 있다. I와 am의 축약형은 I'm이고, She, It과 is의 축약형은 She's, It's이며, You와 are의 축약형은 You're이다.

문법 쏙쏙
pp.12~13

A

1 is	**2** are	**3** am
4 is	**5** is	**6** are
7 is	**8** is	**9** are
10 is	**11** are	**12** is
13 is	**14** is	**15** are

해설

1, 7, 12 > She, It, He가 취하는 be동사는 is이다.
2 > We가 취하는 be동사는 are이다.
3 > I가 취하는 be동사는 am이다.
4, 5, 8, 10, 13, 14 > 주어가 단수이므로 be동사는 is를 쓴다.
6, 9, 11 > 주어가 복수이므로 be동사는 are를 쓴다.
15 > John and I는 주어가 둘 이상이므로 be동사는 are를 쓴다.

B

1 They're	**2** It's	**3** She's
4 It's	**5** They're	**6** I'm
7 He's	**8** It's	**9** We're
10 He's	**11** She's	**12** They're
13 We're	**14** It's	**15** You're

해설

1, 5, 12 > They와 are의 축약형은 They're이다.
2, 4, 8, 14 > It과 is의 축약형은 It's이다.
3, 7, 10, 11 > He, She와 is의 축약형은 He's, She's이다.
6 > I와 am의 축약형은 I'm이다.
9, 13 > We와 are의 축약형은 We're이다.
15 > You와 are의 축약형은 You're이다.

영작 술술
pp.14~15

A

1 I **am** very hungry.
2 Thank you. You **are** so kind.
3 He **is** a famous musician.
4 She **is** a police officer.
5 They **are** from Sydney.
6 James and Susan **are** in the garden.
7 Summer **is** my favorite season.
8 You **are** tall and handsome.
9 The puppies **are** cute.
10 Tom **is** Ann's brother.

B

1 I am tired and sleepy.
2 They are from Spain.
3 She and I are 15 years old.
4 He is a high school student.
5 They are good dancers.
6 He is a pilot.
7 Monkeys are clever.
8 You are my angel.
9 We are at the movie theater.
10 Sue and Emily are sisters.

WRAP **UP**
pp.16~17

A

1 You are a good friend.
2 We are at home.
3 She's 12 years old.
4 Her brother is very tall.
5 They're in the park.
6 Michael is a dentist.
7 Spiders are scary.

해설

1 ▶ You가 취하는 be동사는 are이다.

2 ▶ We가 취하는 be동사는 are이다.

3 ▶ She가 취하는 be동사는 is이고 축약형은 She's이다.

4, 6 ▶ 주어가 단수이므로 be동사는 is를 쓴다.

5 ▶ They가 취하는 be동사는 are이고 축약형은 They're이다.

7 ▶ 주어가 복수이므로 be동사는 are를 쓴다.

B

1 We are from Korea.

2 She is small and cute.

3 Steve and I are at the party.

4 Cheetahs are fast.

5 It is my favorite song.

C 1 ③ 2 ①

해설

1 ▶ My cousins는 복수 주어이므로 be동사는 are를 쓴다.

2 ▶ 각 문장의 주어 James와 He는 모두 단수 주어이므로 be동사 is를 써야 한다.

개념 Review

❶ ~이다 ❷ (~에) 있다 ❸ am

❹ is ❺ are ❻ are

UNIT 02 be동사의 현재형: 부정문/의문문

PRACTICE 1
p.18

1 He is not[isn't] lazy.

2 It is not[isn't] my cellphone.

3 We are not[aren't] in the kitchen.

4 They are not[aren't] friends.

해설

be동사의 부정문은 be동사 뒤에 not을 붙여서 만든다.

PRACTICE 2
p.19

1 Is she a nurse?

2 Are you thirsty?

3 Is the house big?

4 Are they at the library?

해설

be동사의 의문문은 주어와 be동사의 순서를 바꾸고, 문장 끝에 물음표(?)를 붙여서 만든다.

문법 쏙쏙
pp.20~21

A

1 It is not[isn't] an easy question.

2 He is not[isn't] kind to people.

3 I am not[I'm not] afraid of snakes.

4 She is not[isn't] at school now.

5 They are not[aren't] interested in movies.

6 The window is not[isn't] open.

7 The books are not[aren't] on the table.

8 The sun is not[isn't] bright today.

9 Your birthday is not[isn't] in April.

10 Ann is not[isn't] good at singing.

해설

be동사의 부정문은 be동사 뒤에 not을 붙여서 만든다.

B

1 Are the shoes too big?

2 Is the diamond ring expensive?

3 Are tomatoes vegetables?

4 Is the milk in the refrigerator?

5 Are you a soccer fan?

6 Is she still in bed?

7 Are we late for the movie?

9 Is the post office open on Saturdays?

9 Is Italy famous for operas?

10 Is your brother's name Chris?

해설

be동사의 의문문은 주어와 be동사의 순서를 바꾸고, 문장 끝에 물음표(?)를 붙여서 만든다.

영작 술술
pp.22~23

A

1 Is she your friend?

2 I am not interested in sports.

3 It is not your fault.

4 Am I right or wrong?

5 The movie is not interesting.

6 Are they from Australia?

7 He is not in the living room.

8 Are you free now?

9 Are your parents strict?

10 Paul and I are not in the same class.

1 The keys are not[aren't] on the table.

2 Is your bag blue?

3 I am not[I'm not] a liar.

4 They are not[aren't] married.

5 Are you afraid of dogs?

6 She is not[isn't] a fast runner.

7 This box is not[isn't] heavy.

8 We are not[aren't] thirsty.

9 Are Mina and Susie sisters?

10 Is her name Kate?

WRAP UP

pp.24~25

A

1 Is he kind to children?

2 Joe is not[isn't] fat.

3 Is Susan angry with me?

4 Elephants are not[aren't] light.

5 Are they twins?

6 I am not a good dancer.

7 Don't worry. You are not[aren't] alone.

해설

1 ▶ be동사의 의문문은 「Be동사+주어 ~?」 형태이므로 Is he로 고쳐야 알맞다.

2 ▶ be동사의 부정문은 「be동사+not」 형태이므로 is not[isn't]이 알맞다.

3 ▶ Susan은 단수 주어이므로 be동사를 Is로 고쳐야 알맞다.

4 ▶ Elephants는 복수 주어이므로 are not[aren't]으로 고쳐야 알맞다.

5 ▶ they가 취하는 be동사는 are이므로 Are they로 고쳐야 알맞다.

6 ▶ I 뒤에 '~이다'라는 뜻의 be동사 am이 빠져 있다. 부정문이므로 am not으로 고쳐야 알맞다.

7 ▶ You가 취하는 be동사는 are이므로 are not[aren't]으로 고쳐야 알맞다.

B

1 Is Amy sick today?

2 They are not[aren't] 15 years old.

3 John and Amy are not[aren't] at the library.

4 Is the museum open on Sundays?

5 Is your father a teacher?

C **1** ② **2** ④

해설

1 ▶ I am not은 I'm not으로 줄여 쓸 수 있다. 하지만 am과 not

은 줄여 쓸 수 없으므로 I amn't는 알맞지 않다.

2 ▶ be동사의 의문문은 「be동사+주어 ~?」 형태이다. Carl and Lily는 복수이므로 be동사는 Are를 쓴다.

개념 Review

❶ not ❷ isn't ❸ aren't

❹ 주어 ❺ 물음표(?)

ACTUAL TEST

pp.26~27

01 ④ **02** ① **03** ③

04 I am not[I'm not] good at cooking.

05 Is your English teacher from Canada?

06 ② **07** ④ **08** ④ **09** ①

10 They are in the classroom.

11 China is not[isn't] a small country.

12 ③ **13** ②

14 He is not my math teacher

15 Are you the only child in your family

해설

01 Whales와 Clara and Stella는 복수 주어이므로 are가 알맞다.

02 My grandmother와 The man은 단수 주어이므로 is가 알맞다.

03 They are의 축약형은 They're이다.

04 be동사의 부정문은 「be동사+not」 형태이다.

05 be동사의 의문문은 「be동사+주어 ~?」 형태이다.

06 The stadium은 단수 주어이므로 is가 주어 뒤에 온다.

07 penguins는 복수 주어이므로 are를 쓰고, 의문문이므로 are가 주어 앞에 온다.

08 be동사 의문문의 대답은 「Yes, 주어+be동사」 또는 「No, 주어+be동사+not」 형태이다. they가 취하는 be동사는 are이고, 부정의 대답이므로 'No, they aren't.'로 대답해야 한다.

09 '너는(you)'으로 질문했으므로 '나는(I)'으로 대답해야 자연스럽다. 주어 I가 취하는 be동사는 am이고, 긍정의 대답이므로 'Yes, I am.'으로 대답해야 한다.

10 '그들'은 They이고, They가 취하는 be동사는 are이다.

11 China는 단수 주어이므로 is를 쓰고, 부정문이므로 is 뒤에 not을 붙인다. is not은 isn't로 줄여 쓸 수 있다.

12 ③ Brian은 단수 주어이므로 are를 is로 고쳐야 알맞다.

13 ② the boys는 복수 주어이므로 Is를 Are로 고쳐야 알맞다.

14 부정문이므로 주어 He 다음에 is가 오고 그 뒤에 not이 온다.

15 의문문이므로 문장 맨 앞에 Are가 오고 그 뒤에 주어 you가 온다.

UNIT **01** 일반동사의 현재형: 긍정문

PRACTICE **1**
p.30

1 watch	**2** wear
3 eats	**4** sleeps

해설

일반동사 현재형의 긍정문은 주어가 3인칭 단수(He, My cat)일 때 동사원형 뒤에 -s/es를 붙인다.

PRACTICE **2**
p.31

1 sleeps	**2** talks
3 watches	**4** brushes
5 makes	**6** flies
7 buys	**8** has

해설

1, 2, 5 ▸ 대부분의 동사는 뒤에 -s를 붙여 3인칭 단수형을 만든다.

3, 4 ▸ -ch, -sh로 끝나는 동사는 뒤에 -es를 붙인다.

6 ▸ 「자음+y」로 끝나는 동사는 y를 i로 고치고 -es를 붙인다.

7 ▸ 「모음+y」로 끝나는 동사는 그대로 뒤에 -s를 붙인다.

8 ▸ have는 불규칙 동사로 has로 바꾼다.

문법 쏙쏙
pp.32~33

A

1 drives	**2** love	**3** opens
4 go	**5** has	**6** have
7 play	**8** walk	**9** lives
10 leaves	**11** like	**12** costs
13 forgets	**14** exercises	**15** go

해설

1, 3, 9, 10, 12, 13, 14 ▸ 주어가 3인칭 단수이므로 동사에 -s/es를 붙인다.

2, 4, 7, 8, 15 ▸ 주어가 복수이므로 동사에 -s/es를 붙이지 않는다.

5 ▸ Mary는 3인칭 단수이므로 have 대신 has를 쓴다.

6, 11 ▸ 주어가 You, I이므로 동사에 -s/es를 붙이지 않는다.

B

1 closes	**2** works	**3** enjoy
4 do	**5** cry	**6** help

7 studies	**8** washes	**9** go
10 has	**11** like	**12** reads
13 teaches	**14** brushes	**15** get

해설

1, 2, 12 ▸ 주어가 3인칭 단수이므로 동사에 -s/es를 붙인다.

3, 5, 6, 9, 11 ▸ 주어가 복수이므로 동사에 -s/es를 붙이지 않는다.

4, 15 ▸ 주어가 I이므로 동사에 -s/es를 붙이지 않는다.

7 ▸ 주어가 3인칭 단수일 때 「자음+y」로 끝나는 동사는 y를 i로 고치고 -es를 붙인다.

8, 13, 14 ▸ 주어가 3인칭 단수일 때 -sh, -ch로 끝나는 동사는 뒤에 -es를 붙인다.

10 ▸ The singer는 3인칭 단수이므로 have대신 has를 쓴다.

영작 술술
pp.34~35

A

1 They <u>live</u> in Busan.

2 I <u>get</u> up late on Sunday morning.

3 Mike <u>goes</u> to bed at 11 p.m.

4 Grace <u>drinks</u> coffee every morning.

5 Bob <u>reads</u> the newspaper every day.

6 He usually <u>stays</u> at home on weekends.

7 My family and I <u>watch</u> TV in the evening.

8 She <u>meets</u> her friends every Friday.

9 I <u>have</u> a dog, and it <u>eats</u> a lot.

10 He <u>listens</u> to the radio in the car.

B

1 Kate speaks Spanish very well.

2 John teaches math at school.

3 Cats like fish.

4 She gets up early in the morning.

5 He usually skips breakfast.

6 Betty goes to bed at 10 o'clock.

7 We play soccer in the park.

8 I do my homework after school.

9 Sam has a nice computer.

10 They watch TV in the evening.

WRAP **UP**
pp.36~37

A

1 Sally does her homework.

2 I go to school every day.

3 My dad cooks very well.

4 You read a lot of books.

5 Students like Mr. Kim.

6 The house has a large window.

7 Paul and Liz live in the city.

해설

1 ▶ Sally는 3인칭 단수이므로 does가 알맞다.

2, 4 ▶ 주어가 I, You이므로 동사에 -s/es를 붙이지 않는다.

3 ▶ My dad는 3인칭 단수이므로 cooks가 알맞다.

5, 7 ▶ 주어가 복수이므로 동사에 -s/es를 붙이지 않는다.

6 ▶ The house는 3인칭 단수이므로 have 대신 has를 쓴다.

B

1 My grandmother likes flowers.

2 We clean the house on weekends.

3 Peter drives a bus.

4 She has two cats.

5 The bank closes at 4:00 p.m.

C　　**1** ③　　　　　**2** ③

해설

1 ▶ ① studys → studies, ② forget → forgets, ④ plays → play로 고쳐야 알맞다.

2 ▶ Ms. Taylor는 3인칭 단수이므로 comes가 알맞다. usually는 '보통, 평소에'라는 뜻으로 일반동사 앞에 위치하므로 usually comes라고 써야 알맞다.

개념 Review

❶ 3인칭 단수　　　　**❷** -es

❸ i　　　　　　　　**❹** has

UNIT **02** 일반동사의 현재형: 부정문/의문문

PRACTICE **1**　　　　　　　　　　p.38

1 don't like　　　　**2** doesn't have

3 don't go　　　　　**4** doesn't wear

해설

일반동사 현재형의 부정문은 동사 앞에 don't[do not]를 넣고, 주어가 3인칭 단수이면 doesn't[does not]를 넣는다. 이때 뒤에 오는 동사는 항상 원형을 쓴다.

PRACTICE **2**　　　　　　　　　　p.39

1 Do, play　　　　　**2** Does, take

3 Does, walk　　　　**4** Do, need

해설

일반동사 현재형의 의문문은 「Do/Does+주어+동사원형 ~?」 형태이다. 주어가 3인칭 단수이면 Do 대신 Does를 사용한다.

문법 쑥쑥　　　　　　　　　　　pp.40~41

A

1 don't, like　　　　**2** doesn't, have

3 Do, go　　　　　　**4** Does, freeze

5 doesn't, work　　**6** don't, want

7 doesn't, live　　　**8** doesn't, taste

9 Do, live　　　　　**10** Does, run

11 doesn't, eat　　　**12** Does, cry

13 Do, have　　　　**14** don't, grow

15 Does, have

해설

1, 6, 14 ▶ 주어가 I, you, we, they, 복수 명사이면 「don't+동사원형」 형태로 부정문을 만든다.

2, 5, 7, 8, 11 ▶ 주어가 3인칭 단수이면 「doesn't+동사원형」 형태로 부정문을 만든다.

3, 9, 13 ▶ 주어가 I, you, we, they, 복수 명사이면 「Do+주어+동사원형 ~?」 형태로 의문문을 만든다.

4, 10, 12, 15 ▶ 주어가 3인칭 단수이면 「Does+주어+동사원형 ~?」 형태로 의문문을 만든다.

B

1 don't go / Do, go

2 doesn't have / Does, have

3 doesn't live / Does, live

4 don't know / Do, know

5 don't work / Do, work

6 doesn't have / Does, have

7 doesn't sell / Does, sell

해설

1, 4, 5 ▶ 주어가 you, they이므로 부정문은 「don't+동사원형」, 의문문은 「Do+주어+동사원형 ~?」 형태이다.

2, 3, 6, 7 ▶ 주어가 3인칭 단수이므로 부정문은 「doesn't+동사원형」, 의문문은 「Does+주어+동사원형 ~?」 형태이다.

영작 술술　　　　　　　　　　　pp.42~43

A

1 <u>Do</u> <u>you</u> <u>like</u> K-pop?

2 The store <u>doesn't</u> <u>sell</u> fruit.

3 <u>Does</u> the train <u>leave</u> in thirty minutes?

4 <u>Do</u> they <u>walk</u> to school?

5 Brian doesn't ride a motorcycle.

6 Does she wear glasses?

7 Mike and I don't meet very often.

8 I don't play the piano.

9 The girl doesn't have long hair.

10 Does your mom drive a car?

B

1 I don't have a problem.

2 We don't know each other.

3 Do you like Italian food?

4 Does she live in Korea?

5 He doesn't have a brother.

6 They don't enjoy skiing.

7 Do you need a pen?

8 The computer doesn't work well.

9 Does Tom speak Korean?

10 Do they have a pet?

WRAP UP

pp.44~45

A

1 Do you like classical music?

2 My father doesn't[does not] drive a car.

3 Does she go to college?

4 Tim doesn't have a bike.

5 Does it smell good?

6 They don't[do not] do their homework.

7 I don't[do not] like onions.

해설

1 ▶ 일반동사 현재형의 의문문은 「Do/Does+주어+동사원형 ~?」 형태이다. 주어가 you이므로 Do you로 고쳐야 알맞다.

2 ▶ My father는 3인칭 단수이므로 doesn't[does not] drive 로 고쳐야 알맞다.

3 ▶ 일반동사 현재형의 의문문은 「Do/Does+주어+동사원형 ~?」 형태이므로 Does she go로 고쳐야 알맞다.

4 ▶ doesn't 뒤에는 동사원형이 와야 하므로 doesn't have로 고쳐야 알맞다.

5 ▶ it은 3인칭 단수이므로 Does it으로 고쳐야 알맞다.

6 ▶ 일반동사 현재형의 부정문은 「don't/doesn't+동사원형」 형태이다. 주어가 They이므로 don't[do not] do로 고쳐야 알맞다.

7 ▶ 일반동사 현재형의 부정문은 「don't/doesn't+동사원형」 형태이다. 주어가 I이므로 don't[do not] like로 고쳐야 알맞다.

B

1 Do you meet your friends every day?

---

2 Does she like music?

3 I don't[do not] know his phone number.

4 He doesn't[does not] eat instant noodles.

5 Does the school festival start on Friday?

C **1** ① **2** ③

해설

1 ▶ Mike는 3인칭 단수이므로 don't를 doesn't로 고쳐야 알맞다.

2 ▶ 주어가 She이므로 일반동사 현재형의 부정문은 「doesn't+동사원형」, 의문문은 「Does+주어+동사원형 ~?」 형태이다.

개념 Review

❶ don't(= do not) **❷** doesn't(= does not)

❸ 원형 **❹** Do

❺ Does **❻** 원형

ACTUAL TEST

pp.46~47

01 ③ **02** ③ **03** ③ **04** ④

05 ② **06** ③ **07** ② **08** ④

09 He wears a suit every day.

10 My parents don't enjoy sporting events.

11 Does she often go to the movies?

12 ④ **13** ③

14 Susan doesn't watch TV every day.

15 Does the train arrive on time?

해설

01 동사 take에 -s가 붙어있으므로 주어는 3인칭 단수형인 The girl이 알맞다.

02 ③ 「자음+y」로 끝나는 동사는 y를 i로 고치고 -es를 붙인 다. cry → cries

03 주어가 I일 때 일반동사 현재형의 부정문은 「don't+동사원 형」 형태이다.

04 주어가 3인칭 단수(He)일 때 일반동사 현재형의 부정문은 「doesn't+동사원형」 형태이다.

05 주어가 복수(The kids)일 때 일반동사 현재형의 의문문은 「Do+주어+동사원형 ~?」 형태이다.

06 주어가 3인칭 단수(Jerry)일 때 일반동사 현재형의 의문문 은 「Does+주어+동사원형 ~?」 형태이다.

07 주어가 They일 때 일반동사 현재형의 부정문은 「don't+ 동사원형」 형태이다.

08 ④ your father는 3인칭 단수이므로 Do를 Does로 고쳐 야 알맞다.

09 주어가 He이므로 동사 wear는 wears가 된다.

10 주어가 복수(My parents)일 때 일반동사 현재형의 부정문 은 「don't+동사원형」 형태이다.

11 주어가 3인칭 단수(She)일 때 일반동사 현재형의 의문문은 「Does+주어+동사원형 ~?」 형태이다.

12 주어가 3인칭 단수(Kate)일 때 일반동사 현재형의 부정문은 「doesn't+동사원형」 형태이다.

13 주어가 you일 때 일반동사 현재형의 의문문은 「Do+주어+동사원형 ~?」 형태이다.

14 주어가 3인칭 단수(Susan)일 때 일반동사 현재형의 부정문은 「doesn't+동사원형」 형태이다.

15 Do/Does가 쓰인 의문문에서 일반동사(arrive)는 반드시 원형을 쓴다.

Chapter 03 현재진행형

UNIT 01 현재진행형: 긍정문

PRACTICE 1
p.50

1 is wearing	2 am listening
3 is playing	4 are drinking

해설

현재진행형은 「am/is/are+동사원형-ing」 형태이다. 주어에 알맞은 be동사를 선택하고 동사에 -ing를 붙이면 된다.

PRACTICE 2
p.51

1 cooking	2 reading	3 jogging
4 sitting	5 smiling	6 flying
7 lying	8 passing	

해설

1, 2, 8 ▶ 대부분의 동사는 동사원형에 -ing를 붙인다.
3, 4 ▶ 「단모음+단자음」으로 끝나는 동사는 자음을 한 번 더 쓰고 -ing를 붙인다.
5 ▶ -e로 끝나는 동사는 e를 빼고 -ing를 붙인다.
6 ▶ -y로 끝나는 동사는 그대로 -ing를 붙인다.
7 ▶ -ie로 끝나는 동사는 ie를 y로 고치고 -ing를 붙인다.

문법 쏙쏙
pp.52~53

A

1 eating	2 cleaning	3 throwing
4 sitting	5 studying	6 waving
7 dying	8 waiting	9 writing
10 playing	11 watching	12 swimming

13 talking　　14 standing　　15 having

해설

1, 2, 3, 8, 11, 13, 14 ▶ 대부분의 동사는 동사원형에 -ing를 붙인다.
4, 12 ▶ 「단모음+단자음」으로 끝나는 동사는 자음을 한 번 더 쓰고 -ing를 붙인다.
5, 10 ▶ -y로 끝나는 동사는 그대로 -ing를 붙인다.
6, 9, 15 ▶ -e로 끝나는 동사는 e를 빼고 -ing를 붙인다.
7 ▶ -ie로 끝나는 동사는 ie를 y로 고치고 -ing를 붙인다.

B

1 The phone is ringing.
2 The girl is smiling.
3 The man is working hard.
4 You are eating a sandwich for lunch.
5 Mary is buying milk at the supermarket.
6 The workers are cutting the trees.
7 He is sending an email.
8 The dog is lying on the floor.
9 My brother is riding his bicycle.
10 The airplane is flying above the clouds.

해설

1, 3, 7 ▶ 현재진행형은 「am/is/are+동사원형-ing」 형태이다. 주어가 단수이므로 is를 쓰고, 동사원형에 -ing를 붙인다.
2, 9 ▶ 주어가 단수이므로 is를 쓰고, -e로 끝나는 동사는 e를 빼고 -ing를 붙인다.
4 ▶ 주어가 You이므로 are를 쓰고, 동사원형에 -ing를 붙인다.
5, 10 ▶ 주어가 단수이므로 is를 쓰고, -y로 끝나는 동사는 그대로 -ing를 붙인다.
6 ▶ 주어가 복수이므로 are를 쓰고, 「단모음+단자음」으로 끝나는 동사는 자음을 한 번 더 쓰고 -ing를 붙인다.
8 ▶ 주어가 단수이므로 is를 쓰고, -ie로 끝나는 동사는 ie를 y로 고치고 -ing를 붙인다.

영작 술술
pp.54~55

A

1 Jisu is taking an English exam.
2 Mom is doing the dishes.
3 Sam and Emily are playing a board game.
4 Ken is talking to his doctor.
5 He is using his computer.
6 The students are studying at the library.
7 Kate is shopping online.
8 They are having dinner at a restaurant.
9 The girl is wearing her school uniform.
10 Brian is running with his dog.

1 I am eating pasta.

2 Susan is cooking in the kitchen.

3 The boy is flying a kite.

4 Mike is talking on the phone.

5 We are lying on the beach.

6 They are swimming in the pool.

7 Sarah is wearing sunglasses.

8 He is playing games on his cellphone.

9 Chris and I are doing our homework.

10 They are enjoying their vacation.

WRAP UP

pp.56~57

A

1 is baking	2 am having
3 are speaking	4 is walking
5 are drinking	6 is washing

해설

1 ▶ 현재진행형은 「am/is/are+동사원형-ing」 형태이다. '컵케이크를 굽다'는 bake cupcakes이다.

2 ▶ '아침 식사를 하다'는 have breakfast이다.

3 ▶ '영어를 말하다'는 speak English이다.

4 ▶ '학교에 걸어가다'는 walk to school이다.

5 ▶ '오렌지 주스를 마시다'는 drink orange juice이다.

6 ▶ '머리를 감다'는 wash one's hair이다.

B

1 Beth is watering the flowers.

2 They are sitting on the grass.

3 I am brushing my teeth.

4 She is wearing a wedding ring.

5 Joe is texting his friend.

C 　　1 ③　　　　2 ③

해설

1 ▶ ③ run은 「단모음+단자음」으로 끝나므로 are runing → are running으로 고쳐야 알맞다.

2 ▶ '~하고 있다, ~하는 중이다'라는 의미의 현재진행형은 「am/is/are+동사원형-ing」 형태이다. 동사 write의 -ing형은 writing이므로 ③이 알맞다.

개념 Review

❶ 「am/is/are+동사원형-ing」 ❷ a, e, i, o, u
❸ 단모음 ❹ 단자음

UNIT 02 현재진행형: 부정문/의문문

PRACTICE 1

p.58

1 They are not[aren't] singing.

2 The baby is not[isn't] crying.

3 He is not[isn't] eating pizza.

4 We are not[aren't] drawing pictures.

해설

현재진행형 부정문은 「am/is/are+not+동사원형-ing」 형태이다.

PRACTICE 2

p.59

1 Is, opening	2 Are, looking
3 Is, kicking	4 Are, jumping

해설

현재진행형 의문문은 「Am/Is/Are+주어+동사원형-ing ~?」 형태이다.

문법 쏙쏙

pp.60~61

A

1 Is, crossing

2 is not[isn't] fixing

3 Is, cleaning

4 am not chewing

5 Is, climbing

6 Is, biting

7 are not[aren't] sitting

8 Is, working

9 is not[isn't] wearing

10 are not[aren't] studying

11 is not[isn't] swimming

12 Are, thinking

13 Is, feeding

14 are not[aren't] drinking

15 Is, looking

해설

1, 3, 5, 8, 12, 13, 15 ▶ 현재진행형 의문문은 「Am/Is/Are+주어+동사원형-ing ~?」 형태이다.

2, 4, 9, 14 ▶ 현재진행형 부정문은 「am/is/are+not+동사원형-ing」 형태이다.

6 ▶ -e로 끝나는 동사는 e를 빼고 -ing를 붙인다.

7, 11 ▶ 「단모음+단자음」으로 끝나는 동사는 자음을 한 번 더 쓰고 -ing를 붙인다.

10 ▶ -y로 끝나는 동사는 그대로 -ing를 붙인다.

B

1 (부정문) He is not[isn't] playing the guitar.
(의문문) Is he playing the guitar?

2 (부정문) The man is not[isn't] fishing in the river.
(의문문) Is the man fishing in the river?

3 (부정문) She is not[isn't] sleeping in her bedroom.
(의문문) Is she sleeping in her bedroom?

4 (부정문) The children are not[aren't] laughing.
(의문문) Are the children laughing?

5 (부정문) Kevin and Cindy are not[aren't] reading comic books.
(의문문) Are Kevin and Cindy reading comic books?

6 (부정문) The cat is not[isn't] chasing the mouse.
(의문문) Is the cat chasing the mouse?

7 (부정문) Tom is not[isn't] wearing his new T-shirt.
(의문문) Is Tom wearing his new T-shirt?

해설
현재진행형 부정문은 「am/is/are+not+동사원형-ing」 형태이다. 현재진행형 의문문은 「Am/Is/Are+주어+동사원형-ing ~?」 형태이다.

영작 술술
pp.62~63

A

1 Are they staying at the hotel?
2 Sally is not listening to the radio.
3 Are they lying on the beach?
4 I am not doing my homework.
5 Is your sister building a sandcastle?
6 The man is not wearing his shoes.
7 Are you talking to me now?
8 They are not drinking milk.
9 Is she waiting for a bus?
10 Is the fire alarm ringing?

B

1 Is Ann helping her mother?
2 I am not[I'm not] studying English.
3 Is George washing his car?
4 Olivia is not[isn't] closing her eyes.
5 The TV is not[isn't] working at the moment.
6 Are you going to the library?
7 Are they speaking Chinese?

8 She is not[isn't] answering the phone.
9 Are the boys coming home?
10 Jimmy is not[isn't] eating anything.

WRAP UP
pp.64~65

A

1 I am not going to school.
2 The black cat is not[isn't] looking at me.
3 Ann and Mike are not studying.
4 He isn't wearing glasses today.
5 Are you carrying a box?
6 Is she making dinner right now?
7 Are the birds drinking water?

해설
1 ▶ 현재진행형 부정문은 「am/is/are+not+동사원형-ing」 형태이므로 not going으로 고쳐야 알맞다.
2 ▶ 현재진행형 부정문은 「am/is/are+not+동사원형-ing」 형태이므로 is not[isn't]으로 고쳐야 알맞다.
3 ▶ Ann and Mike는 복수 주어이므로 are로 고쳐야 알맞다.
4 ▶ 현재진행형 부정문은 「am/is/are+not+동사원형-ing」 형태이므로 wearing으로 고쳐야 알맞다.
5 ▶ 현재진행형 의문문은 「Am/Is/Are+주어+동사원형-ing ~?」 형태이므로 Are로 고쳐야 알맞다.
6 ▶ 현재진행형 의문문은 「Am/Is/Are+주어+동사원형-ing ~?」 형태이므로 making으로 고쳐야 알맞다.
7 ▶ the birds는 복수 주어이므로 Are로 고쳐야 알맞다.

B

1 He is not[isn't] exercising now.
2 Is Sue practicing the piano?
3 Are you writing a birthday card?
4 I am not[I'm not] listening to music.
5 Are they going to the airport?

C   **1** ④   **2** ④

해설
1 ▶ now가 쓰였으므로 지금 진행 중인 일을 나타낸다. 현재진행형 부정문은 「am/is/are+not+동사원형-ing」이므로 ④ aren't playing이 알맞다.
2 ▶ 현재진행형 의문문은 「Am/Is/Are+주어+동사원형-ing ~?」 형태이므로 ④가 알맞다.

개념 Review

❶ not	❷ isn't
❸ He's	❹ be동사

01 ④   **02** ③

03 The computer is not working at the moment

04 Are they making a lot of noise

05 ③   **06** ④   **07** ④   **08** ④

09 ②   **10** ①   **11** ②   **12** ④

13 ③

14 They are walking to the subway station.

15 Is Jessica planting flowers

해설

01 매일 하는 일은 현재시제로 나타내지만, 지금 진행 중인 일은 현재진행형인 「am/is/are＋동사원형-ing」 형태로 나타낸다.

02 ① eatting → eating, ② danceing → dancing, ④ swiming → swimming으로 고쳐야 알맞다.

03 현재진행형 부정문은 「am/is/are＋not＋동사원형-ing」 형태이다.

04 현재진행형 의문문은 「Am/Is/Are＋주어＋동사원형-ing ～?」 형태이다.

05 ①, ②, ④는 현재진행형으로 빈칸에는 be동사 Are가 알맞다. ③의 every day는 현재시제와 어울리는 시간 표현으로 빈칸에는 Do가 알맞다.

06 현재진행형 부정문은 「am/is/are＋not＋동사원형-ing」 형태이다. 주어가 복수이므로 be동사는 are를 쓴다.

07 현재진행형 의문문은 「Am/Is/Are＋주어＋동사원형-ing ～?」 형태이다. 주어가 복수이므로 be동사는 Are를 쓴다.

08 지금 진행 중인 일은 현재진행형인 「am/is/are＋동사원형 -ing」 형태로 쓴다.

09 현재진행형 의문문은 「Am/Is/Are＋주어＋동사원형-ing ～?」 형태이다.

10 현재진행형 의문문은 「Am/Is/Are＋주어＋동사원형-ing ～?」 형태이고, 일반동사 현재형의 의문문은 「Do/Does＋주어＋동사원형 ～?」 형태이다. 따라서 ①은 Is the rabbit eating ～? 또는 Does the rabbit eat ～?으로 고쳐야 알맞다.

11 ②는 now가 쓰여 의미상 현재진행형이 되어야 하므로 doesn't sleeping을 isn't sleeping으로 고쳐야 알맞다.

12 상대방에게 지금 울고 있는지를 묻고 있다. 현재진행형 의문문은 「Am/Is/Are＋주어＋동사원형-ing ～?」 형태이므로 ④가 알맞다.

13 지금 무엇을 하고 있는지에 대한 대답이므로 현재진행형인 ③ I'm making이 알맞다.

14 현재진행형은 「am/is/are＋동사원형-ing」 형태이다. 주어가 They이므로 are를 써서 'They are walking ～'으로 나타낸다.

15 현재진행형 의문문은 「Am/Is/Are＋주어＋동사원형-ing ～?」 형태이다. Jessica가 단수이므로 is를 써서 'Is Jessica planting flowers ～?'로 나타낸다.

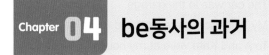

Chapter 04   be동사의 과거

UNIT 01   be동사의 과거형: 긍정문

PRACTICE 1 p.70

1 was   **2** was

3 were   **4** were

해설

be동사의 과거형은 주어가 I, he, she, it, 단수 명사일 때 was, 주어가 we, you, they, 복수 명사일 때 were를 쓴다.

PRACTICE 2 p.71

1 last   **2** yesterday

3 last   **4** ago

해설

yesterday는 단독으로 또는 yesterday morning/afternoon/evening 형태로 쓸 수 있다. last는 '지난～'의 의미이고, ago는 '～ 전에'의 의미이다.

문법 쏙쏙 pp.72~73

A

1 was   **2** were   **3** was

4 were   **5** was   **6** were

7 was   **8** was   **9** were

10 were   **11** was   **12** was

13 was   **14** were   **15** was

해설

1, 3, 5, 7, 8, 11, 12, 13, 15 ▶ 주어가 I, he, she, it, 단수 명사일 때 be동사의 과거형은 was를 쓴다.

2, 4, 6, 10, 14 ▶ 주어가 we, you, they, 복수 명사일 때 be동사의 과거형은 were를 쓴다.

9 ▶ Helen and I는 둘 이상이므로 복수 취급해서 were를 쓴다.

B

1 The box was empty.

2 It was a funny joke.

3 Sam and Sarah were my classmates.

4 Your name was on the waiting list.

5 The clothes were dirty.

6 The traffic was heavy.

7 Tennis was my favorite sport.

8 The car was in the garage.

9 My neighbors were kind and friendly.

10 Tom and Kate were at my house.

해설

be동사 am, is의 과거형은 was를 쓰고, are의 과거형은 were를 쓴다.

영작 술술

pp.74~75

A

1 I <u>was</u> late for school yesterday.

2 They <u>were</u> in Busan last weekend.

3 We <u>were</u> at Andy's house.

4 Mike <u>was</u> on vacation last week.

5 The pants <u>were</u> too big.

6 The dishes <u>were</u> clean.

7 The child <u>was</u> missing two days ago.

8 Ms. Taylor <u>was</u> my English teacher last year.

9 My grandmother <u>was</u> born in 1958.

10 We <u>were</u> at the beach yesterday.

B

1 The soup was hot.

2 We were at the amusement park yesterday.

3 My favorite toy was a teddy bear.

4 I was in elementary school last year.

5 He was a member of the club.

6 We were in London a month ago.

7 His office was on the 7th floor.

8 It was a wonderful experience.

9 Thomas Edison was a great inventor.

10 They were brave soldiers.

WRAP UP

pp.76~77

A

1 He was a famous movie star.

2 The cake was too sweet.

3 They were angry with me.

4 It was a good idea.

5 The rabbits were in the cage.

6 I was at Jane's house.

7 The weather was nice.

해설

1, 2, 4, 6, 7 ▶ am, is의 과거형은 was이다.

3, 5 ▶ are의 과거형은 were이다.

B

1 The door was locked last night.

2 She was absent yesterday.

3 We were at home last weekend.

4 Mark was sick three days ago.

5 The beach was beautiful.

C　　**1**　③　　　　　**2**　③

해설

1 ▶ ③ last year는 과거를 나타내므로 are의 과거형인 were로 고쳐야 알맞다.

2 ▶ 의미상 과거형 문장이고, My apartment는 단수 명사이므로 ③ was를 쓴 문장이 알맞다.

개념 Review

❶ was　　　　　**❷** were

❸ last ~　　　　**❹** ~ ago

UNIT 02 be동사의 과거형: 부정문/의문문

PRACTICE 1

p.78

1 I wasn't[was not] sad yesterday.

2 We weren't[were not] at the zoo.

3 The river wasn't[was not] deep.

4 The bottles weren't[were not] empty.

해설

be동사 과거형의 부정문은 「was/were+not」 형태이고, 각각 wasn't, weren't로 줄여 쓸 수 있다.

PRACTICE 2

p.79

1 Were you born in France?

2 Was he a good student?

3 Was the book expensive?

4 Were they at work yesterday?

해설

be동사 과거형의 의문문은 「Was/Were+주어 ~?」 형태이다.

pp.80~81

A

1 wasn't	**2** wasn't	**3** wasn't
4 Were	**5** wasn't	**6** Were
7 wasn't	**8** Were	**9** wasn't
10 wasn't	**11** Was	**12** Were
13 wasn't	**14** Were	**15** Was

해설

1, 2, 3, 5, 7, 9, 10, 13 ▶ 주어가 I, 단수 명사이므로 wasn't를 쓴다.

4, 6, 8, 12, 14 ▶ 주어가 you, they, 복수 명사이므로 Were를 쓴다.

11, 15 ▶ 주어가 he, 단수 명사이므로 Was를 쓴다.

B

1 (부정문) The party wasn't fun last weekend.
(의문문) Was the party fun last weekend?

2 (부정문) The vase wasn't on the table.
(의문문) Was the vase on the table?

3 (부정문) Mike wasn't your best friend.
(의문문) Was Mike your best friend?

4 (부정문) The car wasn't new.
(의문문) Was the car new?

5 (부정문) The people weren't friendly.
(의문문) Were the people friendly?

6 (부정문) The rumor about him wasn't true.
(의문문) Was the rumor about him true?

7 (부정문) The shops weren't open yesterday.
(의문문) Were the shops open yesterday?

해설

be동사 과거형의 부정문은 「was/were+not」 형태이고, 각각 wasn't, weren't로 줄여 쓸 수 있다. be동사 과거형의 의문문은 「Was /Were+주어 ~?」 형태이다.

영작 술술

pp.82~83

A

1 Was he your favorite singer?

2 The shoes were not expensive.

3 Was your birthday last Friday?

4 Was Jason on vacation last week?

5 Was your dog sick last night?

6 The vegetables were not fresh.

7 The umbrella was not in the car.

8 Were you in 6th grade last year?

9 The movie was not interesting.

10 I was not at Jane's house yesterday.

B

1 It wasn't his wallet.

2 The boxes weren't big enough.

3 Was the game exciting?

4 Were you here last night?

5 The classes weren't difficult.

6 Were they absent yesterday?

7 Were you born in this city?

8 Was the weather cold yesterday?

9 I wasn't happy after the test.

10 The library wasn't open yesterday.

WRAP UP

pp.84~85

A

1 Were you late for the meeting?

2 Jenny was not[wasn't] tired.

3 He was not in class yesterday.

4 We were not[weren't] sure about it.

5 The weather was not[wasn't] warm.

6 Their car wasn't[was not] old.

7 Was the movie good last night?

해설

1 ▶ 주어가 you이므로 Were로 고쳐야 알맞다.

2 ▶ Jenny는 단수 주어이므로 was not[wasn't]으로 고쳐야 알맞다.

3 ▶ yesterday는 과거를 나타내고 주어가 He이므로 was로 고쳐야 알맞다.

4 ▶ be동사 과거형의 부정문은 「was/were+not」 형태이므로 were not[weren't]으로 고쳐야 알맞다.

5 ▶ The weather는 단수 주어이므로 was not[wasn't]으로 고쳐야 알맞다.

6 ▶ Their car는 단수 주어이므로 wasn't[was not]로 고쳐야 알맞다.

7 ▶ last night은 과거를 나타내므로 Was로 고쳐야 알맞다.

B

1 Was it a good trip?

2 The job was not[wasn't] easy.

3 The room was not[wasn't] dark.

4 Were they too noisy last night?

5 Were the chairs comfortable?

해설

1 ▶ the children은 복수 주어이므로 Was를 Were로 고쳐야 알맞다.

2 ▶ be동사 과거형의 부정문은 「was/were+not」 형태이다. be동사 과거형의 의문문은 「Was/Were+주어 ~?」 형태이다.

개념 Review

① not
② wasn't
③ weren't
④ 주어

ACTUAL TEST
pp.86~87

01 ③ **02** ② **03** were
04 ④ **05** ③
06 The cup was not[wasn't] broken.
07 Were the socks in the drawer?
08 ③ **09** ④
10 My math homework was not difficult.
11 Was the music too loud?
12 ④ **13** ③
14 I was not[wasn't] alone.
15 Were they in Europe last summer?

해설

01 첫 번째 빈칸은 Last year가 과거를 나타내므로 was를, 두 번째 빈칸은 Now가 현재를 나타내므로 is가 알맞다.

02 ② next year는 미래를 나타내므로 be동사의 과거형인 were와 함께 쓸 수 없다.

03 an hour ago는 과거를 나타내므로 are의 과거형인 were을 써야 한다.

04 last year는 과거를 나타내고 Ann and I는 복수 주어이므로 동사는 were를 쓴다.

05 last Friday는 과거를 나타내고 your birthday party는 단수 주어이므로 Was로 시작하는 의문문이 알맞다.

06 be동사 과거형의 부정문은 「was/were+not」 형태이고, 각각 wasn't, weren't로 줄여 쓸 수 있다.

07 be동사 과거형의 의문문은 「Was/Were+주어 ~?」 형태이다.

08 어제 오후에 대한 내용이고 주어가 I이므로 was가 알맞다.

09 과거의 일에 대한 내용이고 주어가 We이므로 were가 알맞다.

10 be동사 과거형의 부정문은 주어 뒤에 「was/were+not」의 어순으로 쓴다.

11 be동사 과거형의 의문문은 「Was/Were+주어 ~?」의 어순으로 쓴다.

12 ④ Kate and her mother는 복수 주어이므로 was를 were로 고쳐야 알맞다.

13 ③ your grandmother는 단수 주어이므로 Were를 Was로 고쳐야 알맞다.

14 주어가 I일 때 be동사의 과거형은 was이다. 부정문이므로 'I was not ~'의 어순으로 쓰고, was not은 wasn't로 줄여 쓸 수 있다.

15 주어가 they일 때 be동사의 과거형은 were이다. 의문문이므로 'Were they ~?'의 어순으로 쓴다.

Chapter 05 일반동사의 과거

UNIT 01 일반동사의 과거형: 긍정문

PRACTICE 1
p.90

1 asked **2** helped **3** closed
4 dropped **5** cried **6** stayed
7 finished **8** planned

해설

1, 2, 7 ▶ 대부분의 일반동사는 동사원형에 -ed를 붙여 과거형을 만든다.

3 ▶ -e로 끝나는 동사는 -d만 붙인다.

4, 8 ▶ 「단모음+단자음」으로 끝나는 동사는 자음을 한 번 더 쓰고 -ed를 붙인다.

5 ▶ 「자음+y」로 끝나는 동사는 y를 i로 고치고 -ed를 붙인다.

6 ▶ 「모음+y」로 끝나는 동사는 -ed를 붙인다.

PRACTICE 2
p.91

1 ate **2** went **3** came
4 did **5** ran **6** slept
7 read **8** wrote

해설

일부 동사들은 -ed가 붙여서 과거형이 되지 않고 자신들만의 불규칙한 과거형을 갖는다.

문법 쏙쏙
pp.92~93

A

1 stayed **2** waited **3** lived
4 got **5** took **6** danced
7 had **8** broke **9** dropped
10 ran **11** said **12** slept
13 rode **14** bought **15** made

1 ▷ 「모음+y」로 끝나는 동사는 -ed를 붙인다.

2 ▷ 대부분의 일반동사는 -ed를 붙여 과거형을 만든다.

3, 6 ▷ -e로 끝나는 동사는 -d만 붙인다.

4 ▷ 불규칙 동사인 get의 과거형은 got이다.

5 ▷ 불규칙 동사인 take의 과거형은 took이다.

7 ▷ 불규칙 동사인 have의 과거형은 had이다.

8 ▷ 불규칙 동사인 break의 과거형은 broke이다.

9 ▷ 「단모음+단자음」으로 끝나는 동사는 자음을 한 번 더 쓰고 -ed를 붙인다.

10 ▷ 불규칙 동사인 run의 과거형은 ran이다.

11 ▷ 불규칙 동사인 say의 과거형은 said이다.

12 ▷ 불규칙 동사인 sleep의 과거형은 slept이다.

13 ▷ 불규칙 동사인 ride의 과거형은 rode이다.

14 ▷ 불규칙 동사인 buy의 과거형은 bought이다.

15 ▷ 불규칙 동사인 make의 과거형은 made이다.

B

1 walked	2 had	3 studied
4 came	5 jogged	6 drank
7 did	8 played	9 read
10 saved		

해설

1 ▷ 대부분의 일반동사는 -ed를 붙여 과거형을 만든다.

2 ▷ 불규칙 동사인 have의 과거형은 had이다.

3 ▷ 「자음+y」로 끝나는 동사는 y를 i로 고치고 -ed를 붙인다.

4 ▷ 불규칙 동사인 come의 과거형은 came이다.

5 ▷ 「단모음+단자음」으로 끝나는 동사는 자음을 한 번 더 쓰고 -ed를 붙인다.

6 ▷ 불규칙 동사인 drink의 과거형은 drank이다.

7 ▷ 불규칙 동사인 do의 과거형은 did이다.

8 ▷ 「모음+y」로 끝나는 동사는 -ed를 붙인다.

9 ▷ read[riːd](읽다)의 과거형은 read[red](읽었다)로, 현재형과 과거형의 모양이 같다.

10 ▷ -e로 끝나는 동사는 -d만 붙인다.

영작 술술

pp.94~95

A

1 I <u>turned</u> on the air conditioner.

2 Laura <u>went</u> to Vancouver last summer.

3 Sam <u>painted</u> the house yesterday.

4 We <u>ate</u> pizza and pasta for lunch.

5 Dad <u>helped</u> me with my homework.

6 He <u>gave</u> me a shirt for my birthday.

7 They <u>visited</u> their grandfather two days ago.

8 We <u>enjoyed</u> our trip to Hawaii.

9 Shakespeare <u>wrote</u> Hamlet in 1602.

10 The rain <u>stopped</u> an hour ago.

B

1 I got up late this morning.

2 We went camping last spring.

3 Mike came in first in the race.

4 He slept on the sofa last night.

5 We had lunch together.

6 I met Susie two days ago.

7 They played badminton in the park.

8 The meeting ended at 11 o'clock.

9 He bought a new car last month.

10 The baby cried for an hour.

WRAP UP

pp.96~97

A

1 She traveled to Japan in 2022.

2 He worked at a bank two years ago.

3 I met Jane yesterday.

4 Kim drove to work yesterday.

5 Yesterday, we went to the zoo.

6 They did a lot of work last week.

7 I ran to school yesterday.

해설

1 ▷ in 2022는 과거를 나타내므로 travel의 과거형인 traveled로 고쳐야 알맞다.

2 ▷ two years ago는 과거를 나타내므로 work의 과거형인 worked로 고쳐야 알맞다.

3 ▷ 불규칙 동사인 meet의 과거형은 met이다.

4 ▷ 불규칙 동사인 drive의 과거형은 drove이다.

5 ▷ 불규칙 동사인 go의 과거형은 went이다.

6 ▷ last week는 과거를 나타내므로 do의 과거형인 did로 고쳐야 알맞다.

7 ▷ 불규칙 동사인 run의 과거형은 ran이다.

B

1 I watched a soccer game last night.

2 John missed the school bus this morning.

3 She bought a new house last month.

4 They studied at the library yesterday.

5 I made this cake by myself.

C   1 ②   2 ①

해설

1 ▷ ② 「단모음+단자음」으로 끝나는 동사는 자음을 한 번 더 쓰고 -ed를 붙인다. stoped → stopped

2 ▷ five years ago는 과거를 나타내므로, 불규칙 동사인 write

의 과거형인 ① wrote가 알맞다.

UNIT 02 일반동사의 과거형: 부정문/의문문

PRACTICE 1 p.98

1 didn't change	**2** didn't read
3 didn't go	**4** didn't do

해설
일반동사 과거형의 부정문은 주어에 관계없이 「didn't[did not]+동사원형」 형태로 쓴다.

PRACTICE 2 p.99

1 Did, break	**2** Did, buy
3 Did, go	**4** Did, enjoy

해설
일반동사 과거형의 의문문은 주어에 관계없이 「Did+주어+동사원형 ~?」 형태로 쓴다.

문법 쏙쏙 pp.100~101

A

1 Ann didn't do the dishes after dinner.
2 Sean didn't shave this morning.
3 We didn't like the movie.
4 My English didn't improve a lot last year.
5 I didn't email my sister yesterday.
6 Sally didn't have the flu last week.
7 My father didn't go to work yesterday.
8 Jerry didn't make his bed this morning.
9 I didn't do my history homework last night.
10 They didn't go on a picnic last weekend.

해설
일반동사 과거형의 부정문은 주어에 관계없이 「didn't[did not]+동사원형」 형태로 쓴다.

B

1 Did you watch TV last night?
2 Did Mr. Freeman live in that house?

3 Did she read my diary?
4 Did they take a lot of photos?
5 Did James eat all the cake?
6 Did you borrow my pen?
7 Did Mike come home by taxi?
8 Did your team win the foot volleyball game?
9 Did the teacher erase the board?
10 Did they sell their house?

해설
일반동사 과거형의 의문문은 주어에 관계없이 「Did+주어+동사원형 ~?」 형태로 쓴다.

영작 술술 pp.102~103

A

1 Tim didn't buy the shirt.
2 Did Amy come to the farewell party?
3 Clair didn't finish the housework.
4 He didn't say anything to me.
5 Did you surf the Internet yesterday?
6 Did you water the flowers this morning?
7 Did they go swimming last Sunday?
8 She didn't answer my phone yesterday.
9 Did you hear about the news?
10 Mike didn't eat his vegetables.

B

1 I didn't have time for breakfast.
2 Did you enjoy the trip?
3 He didn't speak English very well.
4 Did they go to bed early?
5 I didn't remember his name.
6 Did you get my text message?
7 Did you check your email?
8 She didn't bring her umbrella.
9 Did you visit the Eiffel Tower in Paris?
10 Did you buy a present for Jane.

WRAP UP pp.104~105

A

1 I did not eat
2 Did she go
3 He did not go

4 Did you understand

5 Did they join

6 Tom didn't tell

7 Did they make

해설
1, 3, 6 ▸ 일반동사 과거형의 부정문은 「didn't[did not]+동사원형」 형태이다.

2, 4, 5, 7 ▸ 일반동사 과거형의 의문문은 「Did+주어+동사원형 ~?」 형태이다.

B

1 Did the firefighter save the girl?

2 He didn't lock the door last night.

3 Did you turn off your cell phone?

4 Sam didn't solve the problem.

5 Did you have a good weekend?

C   **1** ③   **2** ③

해설

1 ▸ 일반동사 과거형의 의문문은 「Did+주어+동사원형 ~?」 형태이므로, ③의 ate를 eat로 고쳐야 알맞다.

2 ▸ 일반동사 과거형의 부정문은 「didn't[did not]+동사원형」, 의문문은 「Did+주어+동사원형 ~?」 형태로 쓴다.

개념 Review

❶ didn't(= did not)   ❷ 원형

❸ Did   ❹ 원형

ACTUAL TEST   pp.106~107

01 ③   **02** ③   **03** ③   **04** ③

05 John didn't[did not] take a taxi to work.

06 Did you meet the teacher yesterday?

07 ②

08 Mina joined the book club two months ago.

09 Olivia did not bring her textbooks to class.

10 ③   **11** ①   **12** ②   **13** ①

14 The movie did not[didn't] end until midnight.

15 Did they arrive at the airport on time?

해설

01 last night은 과거를 나타내므로 go의 과거형인 went가 알맞다.

02 two years ago는 과거를 나타내므로 live의 과거형인 lived가 알맞다.

03 ③ 불규칙 동사인 run의 과거형은 ran이다.

04 30 minutes ago, last night 모두 과거를 나타내므로, stop, come의 과거형인 stopped, came을 쓴다.

05 일반동사 과거형의 부정문은 「didn't[did not]+동사원형」 형태이다. took의 원형은 take이므로 didn't[did not] take가 된다.

06 일반동사 과거형의 의문문은 「Did+주어+동사원형 ~?」 형태이다. met의 원형은 meet이므로 Did you meet ~? 가 된다.

07 과거의 일에 대한 대화이므로 Did로 묻고, make의 과거형인 made를 써서 답한다.

08 일반동사 과거형의 긍정문이므로 「주어+동사의 과거형」 어순으로 쓰고, ago(~ 전에)는 「기간+ago」 형태로 쓴다.

09 일반동사 과거형의 부정문은 주어 뒤에 「didn't[did not]+동사원형」 어순으로 쓴다.

10 ③ 「자음+y」로 끝나는 동사는 y를 i로 고치고 -ed를 붙인다. carry → carried

11 ① didn't 뒤에는 동사원형을 써야 하므로 works를 work로 고쳐야 알맞다.

12 일반동사 과거형의 부정문은 「didn't[did not]+동사원형」 형태이다.

13 일반동사 과거형의 의문문은 「Did+주어+동사원형 ~?」 형태이다.

14 일반동사 과거형의 부정문은 「didn't[did not]+동사원형」 이므로 not did를 did not[didn't]으로 고쳐야 알맞다.

15 일반동사의 과거형의 의문문은 「Did+주어+동사원형 ~?」 이므로 arrived를 arrive로 고쳐야 알맞다.

Chapter **06** 미래시제

UNIT **01** will

PRACTICE **1**   p.110

1 will go   **2** will read

3 will take   **4** will open

해설

미래의 일은 「will+동사원형」 형태로 나타낼 수 있다.

PRACTICE **2**   p.111

1 won't go   **2** won't help

3 Will, watch   **4** Will, come

해설

will의 부정문은 「will not[won't]+동사원형」 형태로 쓴다. will의 의문문은 「Will+주어+동사원형 ~?」 형태로 쓴다.

문법 쏙쏙

A

1 We will go to the beach this summer.
2 The cat will eat the fish.
3 They will write some postcards.
4 I will order pizza for dinner.
5 The sun will shine tomorrow.
6 She will pay the phone bill next week.
7 Susan will wear that dress at the wedding.
8 I will become a scientist in the future.
9 He will keep his promise.
10 I will wash my hair tonight.

해설

will을 사용하여 미래의 일을 나타낼 때는 주어에 관계없이 「will +동사원형」 형태로 쓴다.

B

1 will	2 won't	3 will
4 Will	5 won't	6 will
7 won't	8 will	9 will
10 Will	11 won't	12 will
13 won't	14 will	15 will

해설

1 ▶ '~할게'라고 주어의 의지를 표현할 때는 will을 사용한다.
2 ▶ 셔츠가 비싸다고 했으므로 '나는 그것을 사지 않겠다'라는 내용이 이어져야 자연스럽다.
3 ▶ Sam은 훌륭한 학생이라고 했으므로 '그는 시험에 합격할 것이다'라는 내용이 이어져야 자연스럽다.
4 ▶ 상대방에게 '~할 거야?, ~해 줄래?'라고 질문할 때는 Will you ~?라고 물을 수 있다.
5 ▶ 배가 고프지 않다고 했으므로 '햄버거를 먹지 않을 것이다'라는 내용이 이어져야 자연스럽다.
6 ▶ John은 피곤하다고 했으므로 '그는 오늘 밤에 집에 머물 것이다'라는 내용이 이어져야 자연스럽다.
7 ▶ 너무 늦었다고 했으므로 '제시간에 도착하지 못할 것이다'라는 내용이 이어져야 자연스럽다.
8 ▶ 옷이 젖었다고 했으므로 '옷을 갈아 입을 것이다'라는 내용이 앞에 와야 자연스럽다.
9 ▶ 아프다고 했으므로 '병원에 갈 것이다'라는 내용이 이어져야 자연스럽다.
10 ▶ 미래의 일을 예측하는 의문문이므로 「Will+주어 ~?」 형태로 쓴다.
11 ▶ 시간이 있다고 했으므로 '버스를 놓치지 않을 것이다'라는 내용이 이어져야 자연스럽다.
12 ▶ 걱정 말라고 안심시키는 말 뒤에는 '내가 도와줄게'라는 내용이 이어져야 자연스럽다.
13 ▶ '네 비밀을 말하지 않을게'라고 말해야 하므로 won't를 쓴다.
14 ▶ Jane이 노래를 잘한다고 했으므로 '그녀는 훌륭한 가수가 될 것이다'라는 내용이 이어져야 자연스럽다.

15 ▶ Susan의 현재 나이가 14살이라고 했으므로 '내년에 그녀는 15살이 될 것이다'라는 내용이 이어져야 자연스럽다.

영작 술술

A

1 The train <u>will</u> <u>arrive</u> soon.
2 <u>Will</u> you <u>be</u> at home tomorrow?
3 We <u>will</u> <u>have</u> a great time.
4 She <u>will</u> <u>like</u> your present.
5 I <u>will</u> <u>start</u> jogging tomorrow.
6 He <u>will</u> <u>become</u> a great pianist someday.
7 <u>Will</u> you <u>invite</u> your friends?
8 I <u>will</u> <u>open</u> the door.
9 He <u>won't</u> <u>go</u> to the concert tonight.
10 Tom <u>won't</u> <u>visit</u> his aunt this weekend.

B

1 I will be 15 years old next year.
2 Will you use this computer tomorrow?
3 I will not[won't] eat anything at night.
4 The weather will be cloudy tomorrow.
5 I will call you later.
6 I will not[won't] forget your birthday.
7 You will pass the exam.
8 Will Mike come to the party?
9 Will they help the children?
10 I will not[won't] go out this evening.

WRAP UP

A

1 He will fix the car.
2 The dog will not[won't] bite you.
3 Will you go to the movies?
4 I will read the magazine.
5 Will she listen to music?
6 They will build a house.
7 We will not[won't] be at school.

해설

1, 4, 6 ▶ 미래의 일은 「will+동사원형」 형태로 나타낼 수 있다.
2, 7 ▶ will의 부정문은 「will not[won't]+동사원형」 형태이다.
3, 5 ▶ will의 의문문은 「Will+주어+동사원형 ~?」 형태이다.

18 Grammar Plus Writing Start 1

B

1 I will meet him someday.

2 John will not[won't] be at home tomorrow.

3 The exam will not[won't] be easy.

4 Will he come back at 10 o'clock?

5 Will you cook dinner tonight?

C   **1** ③   **2** ③

해설

1 ▷ ① wills → will, ② ate → eat, ④ are → be로 고쳐야 알맞다. will에는 s가 붙지 않으며, will과 won't 뒤에는 동사원형을 쓴다.

2 ▷ 내일 일에 대해 묻고 있으므로 will을 사용해 「Will+주어+동사원형 ~?」 형태로 질문할 수 있다. will 뒤에는 동사원형을 써야 하므로 ④는 알맞지 않다.

개념 Review

❶ will   **❷** 원형   **❸** not
❹ won't   **❺** 주어

UNIT 02 be going to

PRACTICE 1   p.118

1 am, take   **2** is, learn
3 are, buy   **4** are, finish

해설

미래의 일이나 미리 예정된 계획은 「be going to+동사원형」 형태로 나타낼 수 있다. be동사는 주어에 따라 am, is, are를 사용한다.

PRACTICE 2   p.119

1 am not going to walk
2 are not[aren't] going to sleep
3 Are, going to sing
4 Is, going to make

해설

be going to의 부정문은 「be동사+not+going to+동사원형」 형태이다. be going to의 의문문은 「be동사+주어+going to+동사원형 ~?」 형태이다..

문법 쏙쏙   pp.120~121

A

1 He is going to watch a movie tonight.

2 They are going to wait at the park.

3 Jack is going to play the drums in the band.

4 We are going to sell the furniture.

5 I am going to buy a new smartphone.

6 They are going to travel abroad this year.

7 Fred is going to walk to the station.

8 My parents are going to meet my teacher.

9 The groom is going to sing a song for the bride.

10 Jane and I are going to go shopping this afternoon.

해설

1, 3, 7, 9 ▷ 주어가 3인칭 단수이므로 will을 is going to로 바꾼다.

2, 4, 6, 8, 10 ▷ 주어가 복수이므로 will을 are going to로 바꾼다.

5 ▷ 주어가 I이므로 will을 am going to로 바꾼다.

B

1 (부정문) She is not[isn't] going to do the work.
(의문문) Is she going to do the work?

2 (부정문) You are not[aren't] going to wash the jeans.
(의문문) Are you going to wash the jeans?

3 (부정문) The man is not[isn't] going to be in trouble.
(의문문) Is the man going to be in trouble?

4 (부정문) We are not[aren't] going to miss our plane.
(의문문) Are we going to miss our plane?

5 (부정문) The movie is not[isn't] going to start on time.
(의문문) Is the movie going to start on time?

6 (부정문) The police are not[aren't] going to catch the thief.
(의문문) Are the police going to catch the thief?

7 (부정문) The bridge is not[isn't] going to fall down.
(의문문) Is the bridge going to fall down?

해설

be going to의 부정문은 「be동사+not+going to+동사원형」 형태이다. be going to의 의문문은 「be동사+주어+going to+동사원형 ~?」 형태이다.

pp.122~123

A

1 Are you going to <u>watch</u> TV?

2 The soccer game <u>is</u> going to <u>be</u> exciting.

3 She <u>is</u> <u>not</u> going to <u>keep</u> her promise.

4 Janet <u>is</u> <u>not</u> going to <u>cook</u> this evening.

5 I <u>am</u> <u>not</u> going to <u>have</u> a birthday party.

6 We <u>are</u> <u>not</u> going to <u>talk</u> about it anymore.

7 We <u>are</u> going to <u>go</u> to the museum this Saturday.

8 <u>Are</u> they going to <u>walk</u> to the bus stop?

9 He <u>is</u> <u>not</u> going to <u>help</u> us.

10 <u>Are</u> you going to <u>feed</u> the dog?

B

1 We are going to be busy next week.

2 He is not[isn't] going to buy the hat.

3 Are you going to leave tomorrow?

4 We are not[aren't] going to be late.

5 Are they going to take the train?

6 Is he going to send me a letter?

7 Sarah is going to move next month.

8 Are we going to clean the house?

9 Steve is going to quit his job.

10 I am going to travel to Europe next month.

WRAP UP

pp.124~125

A

1 Carol is going to visit her aunt.

2 I am not[I'm not] going to practice the piano.

3 He is going to get a new job.

4 Are you going to meet him?

5 Is she going to make bread?

6 We are not[aren't] going to take a vacation.

7 Are they going to be busy?

해설

1 ▶ 미래의 일은 be going to를 쓰는 경우 「be going to+동사원형」 형태이다. 주어가 3인칭 단수(Carol)이므로 visits를 is going to visit로 바꾼다.

2 ▶ be going to 부정문은 「be동사+not+going to+동사원형」 형태이다. 주어가 I이므로 'I am not[I'm not] going to practice ~'로 바꾼다.

3 ▶ 주어가 He이므로 gets를 is going to get으로 바꾼다.

4 ▶ be going to 의문문은 「be동사+주어+going to+동사원

형 ~?」 형태이다. 주어가 you이므로 'Are you going to meet ~?'으로 바꾼다.

5 ▶ 주어가 she이고 의문문이므로 'Is she going to make ~?'로 바꾼다.

6 ▶ 주어가 We이고 부정문이므로 don't take를 are not [aren't] going to take로 바꾼다.

7 ▶ Are의 원형은 be이므로 'Are they going to be busy?'가 된다.

B

1 We are going to have fun.

2 He is going to get a haircut.

3 Is she going to call me?

4 I am not[I'm not] going to wait for him.

5 Are you going to do your homework after school?

C   1 ④   2 ②

해설

1 ▶ ①, ②, ③은 「be going to+동사원형」 형태로 '~일 것이다'라는 미래의 의미이고, ④는 「be동사+동사원형-ing」 형태로 '가는 중이다'라는 현재진행의 의미를 갖는다.

2 ▶ be going to 부정문은 「be동사+not+going to+동사원형」 형태이다. be going to의 의문문은 「be동사+주어+going to+동사원형 ~?」 형태이다.

개념 Review

❶ be going to   ❷ 계획
❸ not   ❹ be동사

ACTUAL TEST

pp.126~127

01 ③   02 ③   03 be   04 ③

05 ②   06 ④

07 John will get a new job

08 Sally isn't going to play tennis

09 ①   10 ④   11 ③   12 ②

13 I will take his advice.

14 The test is not[isn't] going to be difficult

15 Is the weather going to be good tomorrow?

해설

01 ▶ '(미래에) ~할 것이다' 또는 '~할게'라고 주어의 의지를 표현할 때는 「will+동사원형」으로 나타낼 수 있다.

02 ▶ '결혼할 것이다'라는 의미의 문장으로, 주어가 We이므로 ③ are going to가 와야 한다.

03 ▶ will 뒤에는 동사원형이 와야 하므로 is의 원형인 be가 온다.

04 미래의 일은 will이나 be going to를 사용해서 나타낸다. 주어가 you이고 의문문이므로 ③ Are you going to가 와야 알맞다.

05 「be going to+동사원형」은 미래의 일을 나타내므로 과거를 나타내는 yesterday는 올 수 없다.

06 ④의 두 번째 문장은 현재진행형으로 '그 아이들은 동물원에 가는 중이다'라는 의미이다. 'The children are going to go to the zoo.'로 고쳐야 알맞다.

07 미래의 일은 will을 쓰는 경우 「will+동사원형」 형태이다.

08 be going to의 부정문은 「be동사+not+going to+동사원형」 형태이다.

09 '우승하지 않을 것이다'라는 미래의 일은 「will not[won't]+동사원형」 형태로 쓴다.

10 be going to의 의문문은 「Be동사+주어+going to+동사원형 ~?」 형태이다.

11 ③ will의 부정문은 「will not[won't]+동사원형」 형태이다. will be not → will not be

12 ② be going to 뒤에는 동사원형을 쓴다. reads → read

13 미래의 일은 will을 쓰는 경우 「will+동사원형」 형태이다.

14 be going to 부정문은 「be동사+not+going to+동사원형」 형태이다. the test가 단수 주어이므로 be동사는 is를 쓴다.

15 be going to 의문문은 「Be동사+주어+going to+동사원형 ~?」 형태이다. the weather가 단수 주어이므로 be동사는 Is를 쓴다.

WORKBOOK ANSWERS

Chapter 01 be동사의 현재

UNIT 01 be동사의 현재형: 긍정문   pp.2~3

A

1 is	2 are
3 is	4 are
5 O	6 is
7 are	8 She's
9 O	10 are
11 is	12 O
13 is	14 They're
15 are	

B

1 We are students.
2 I am 11 years old.
3 Luis is from Mexico.
4 The books are in my bag.
5 It is my favorite food.
6 Madrid is in Spain.
7 You are a good friend.
8 His cat is orange.
9 Dolphins are clever.
10 Daniel and I are at the movie theater.

UNIT 02 be동사의 현재형: 부정문/의문문   pp.4~5

A

1 Are you cold?
2 I am not[I'm not] a teacher.
3 Pablo is not[isn't] my friend.
4 Is he a fast runner?
5 You are not[aren't] late.
6 Is the pen red?
7 Are they interested in art?
8 Our dog is not[isn't] sick.
9 Are your parents at home?
10 The cat is not[isn't] under the bed.

B

1 He is not French.
2 Abby is not my sister.
3 They are not in Seoul.
4 It is not on the table.
5 I am not good at cooking.
6 Are you thirsty?
7 Is Anna your classmate?
8 Are the pants too big?
9 Are we late for school?
10 Are you afraid of the dark?

Chapter 02 일반동사의 현재

UNIT 01 일반동사의 현재형: 긍정문   pp.6~7

A

1 O	2 has
3 brushes	4 exercises
5 O	6 studies
7 sleeps	8 O
9 sings	10 O
11 O	12 opens
13 stays	14 listens
15 does	

B

1 I like ice cream.
2 Debby has a white cat.
3 We cook dinner together.
4 The drone flies high in the sky.
5 Sarah goes shopping on weekends.
6 He teaches English at school.
7 Peter walks his dog every day.
8 The girl plays the piano very well.
9 He drives a blue car.
10 They clean the house every Sunday.

A

1 My cat doesn't like water.

2 My cousins don't live in New York.

3 Does he speak Chinese?

4 Does Steve play the guitar?

5 The house doesn't have a garden.

6 Do they work in this building?

7 My mother doesn't drink coffee.

8 I don't watch TV in the morning.

9 Does Mark go to the gym every day?

10 Do you listen to the radio?

B

1 I don't[do not] like spicy food.

2 He doesn't[does not] have a smartphone.

3 Does Sue dance ballet well?

4 Does it rain a lot here?

5 Chris doesn't[does not] work on weekends.

6 My parents don't[do not] travel often.

7 Do your friends use social media?

8 She doesn't[does not] watch horror movies.

9 Do they study hard for their exams?

10 Do you and Kelly go to the same school?

Chapter 03 현재진행형

UNIT 01 현재진행형: 긍정문 pp.10~11

A

1 am drinking	2 is raining
3 is shining	4 are running
5 is walking	6 is riding
7 are studying	8 is jogging
9 are staying	10 are dying
11 is writing	12 am cutting
13 are playing	14 is kicking
15 are swimming	

B

1 I am having breakfast now.

2 They are watching a movie at home.

3 She is reading a book now.

4 Sarah is doing her homework.

5 They are making a cake.

6 We are buying groceries.

7 He is riding a scooter.

8 The dog is lying in the sun.

9 He is running a marathon.

10 The people are sitting on the floor.

UNIT 02 현재진행형: 부정문/의문문 pp.12~13

A

1 It is not[isn't] snowing outside.

2 Is he running to school?

3 The dog is not[isn't] barking loudly.

4 We are not[aren't] watching the news.

5 Is she painting a picture?

6 I am not[I'm not] exercising at the gym.

7 Are you shopping at the mall?

8 Are Rick and Mary talking on the phone?

9 They are not[aren't] dancing at the party.

10 Am I looking good today?

B

1 We are not going to the beach.

2 Anna is not waiting for the bus.

3 The cows are not eating grass.

4 I am not brushing my teeth.

5 Mom and Dad are not laughing.

6 Is the parrot talking?

7 Are the children playing games?

8 Is Peter carrying a box?

9 Is Alice wearing a new dress?

10 Are you walking down the stairs?

Chapter 04 be동사의 과거

UNIT 01 be동사의 과거형: 긍정문 pp.14~15

A

1 was	2 was
3 were	4 was
5 was	6 was

7 were		**8** was	
9 were		**10** was	
11 were		**12** were	
13 were		**14** was	
15 were			

B

1 They were in Paris last summer.
2 She was my mom's best friend.
3 The cake was delicious.
4 He was my math teacher last year.
5 Beethoven was a great composer.
6 We were on vacation two weeks ago.
7 Jane and Mike were at the mall last Sunday.
8 I was late for school this morning.
9 My parents were busy yesterday.
10 The children were quiet in the library.

UNIT **02** be동사의 과거형: 부정문/의문문　pp.16~17

A

1 The school trip wasn't enjoyable.
2 We weren't happy after the game.
3 Was it good news?
4 Was Mr. Smith a good teacher?
5 She wasn't at the party last night.
6 He wasn't interested in the book.
7 Were you at home all day yesterday?
8 Were the pants on sale?
9 They weren't in the office on Friday.
10 Were the gloves in your coat pockets?

B

1 The movie wasn't very scary.
2 She wasn't a teacher last year.
3 The pens weren't in the pencil case.
4 I wasn't tired this morning.
5 The restaurant wasn't crowded yesterday.
6 Was the lesson too difficult?
7 Was the store open last Monday?
8 Were they happy with the results?
9 Was the book interesting?
10 Were you here 10 minutes ago?

Chapter **05**　일반동사의 과거

UNIT **01** 일반동사의 과거형: 긍정문　pp.18~19

A

1 watched		**2** jumped	
3 danced		**4** carried	
5 painted		**6** planned	
7 stopped		**8** enjoyed	
9 broke		**10** took	
11 drove		**12** drank	
13 ate		**14** rode	
15 wrote			

B

1 The girl smiled at me.
2 Isabel played the piano at the concert.
3 He studied English for two hours.
4 My mom hugged me tightly.
5 We went swimming at the beach.
6 Pedro bought a new smartphone last week.
7 They slept in a tent last night.
8 I read some comic books yesterday.
9 He said goodbye to his friends.
10 The students got off the bus.

UNIT **02** 일반동사의 과거형: 부정문/의문문　pp.20~21

A

1 We didn't go to the beach yesterday.
2 Did Mr. Brown drink coffee?
3 I didn't meet Louis at the restaurant.
4 They didn't do the laundry yesterday.
5 Did he move to San Francisco?
6 Did Emma quit her job last week?
7 We didn't eat ice cream for dessert.
8 Did Jeff ride the roller coaster?
9 I didn't buy onions at the supermarket.
10 Did she win first prize at the contest?

B

1 Nick didn't buy a new laptop.
2 The baby didn't take a nap.
3 I didn't feel tired this morning.
4 He didn't bring his wallet.

5 She didn't say anything to me.

6 Did Carol catch a cold?

7 Did Hans fight with his friend?

8 Did you do your homework?

9 Did they grow up in England?

10 Did the class start at 9:30?

Chapter 06 미래시제

UNIT 01 will
pp.22~23

A

1 will meet

2 will eat

3 will take

4 will not[won't] wait

5 Will you become

6 Will they have

7 will not[won't] rain

8 Will you play

9 will be

10 will not[won't] talk

11 will feel

12 will not[won't] go

13 Will she use

14 Will people live

15 will not[won't] watch

B

1 They will plant flowers next spring.

2 Betty will be busy next week.

3 We will go to the airport by taxi.

4 I will help my friend with his homework.

5 We won't have a test on Monday.

6 I will visit you next weekend.

7 They won't be at home tomorrow.

8 Will the concert start soon?

9 Will you go to the wedding on Saturday?

10 Will Mary graduate from college next year?

UNIT 02 be going to
pp.24~25

A

1 I am going to go to the dentist tomorrow.

2 Mr. Green is going to teach us next semester.

3 Bob and Kate are going to see a movie tonight.

4 My brother is going to take his driving test tomorrow.

5 She is not[isn't] going to buy that expensive dress.

6 We are not[aren't] going to see each other for a while.

7 They are not[aren't] going to travel abroad this summer.

8 Are you going to go shopping tomorrow?

9 Is he going to be late for the meeting?

10 Are they going to get married soon?

B

1 The plane is going to take off in half an hour.

2 Her baby is going to be born in July.

3 He is going to work in Japan for a year.

4 Alex and Mia are going to paint the room.

5 Eric is not going to go surfing tomorrow.

6 I am not going to watch TV tonight.

7 We are not going to play tennis today.

8 Is the train going to arrive soon?

9 Are they going to move to a bigger house?

10 Is he going to buy a new scooter?

Grammar Plus Writing

START